SIMPLY MEXICAN

SIMPLY MEXICAN

Lourdes Castro

PHOTOGRAPHY BY
Lucy Schaeffer

TEN SPEED PRESS
Berkeley | Toronto

Contents

Introduction

When people ask me what I do for a living, my response is "I teach people how to cook." Reactions vary but most people are intrigued because even if cooking isn't their "thing," it is for someone close to them, say, a spouse or a parent. I hear comments like "Oh, I love to cook," "I can watch cooking shows all day long," and then there is always the "I wish I could learn.... Do you think you can teach me?" My answer is always the same "Of course I can. It's simple."

Although they may not say it, I know they're thinking "Yeah, right. Cooking is anything but easy." My own sister can't walk into a market without feeling a rise in her pulse rate—not because she's so excited, but because she starts to panic. Overwhelmed and intimidated, she never knows where to begin. But I maintain that cooking is simple. It's not always quick and it may require some understanding, but at its core it is simple.

I like to joke that I developed an interest in cooking because my mother was such a terrible cook. But my career began when I chose to pursue a degree in nutrition at NYU through a department that was then called Nutrition and Restaurant Management. My mother wanted to know what in the world I was going to do with that degree. That was in the early 90s and the food culture back then was not the dynamic, addictive, and thriving industry we know today. It didn't matter; I was hooked. I became a student of food. Eventually the student became the teacher, and I built a career around culinary education, teaching at universities and culinary schools. I even established my own recreational cooking school, which I eventually sold.

Throughout my years teaching, I noticed that there are certain cuisines and techniques that students always request. Next to knife skills (which is definitely the most popular), Mexican food—or rather, *authentic* Mexican food—is what I get asked for the most. Reasons vary. Some students have taken recent trips to Mexico that introduced them to the genuine flavors of the cuisine and sparked their interest in learning about it (I have taken many such trips). Others are second- or third-generation Mexican-Americans who want to recreate the authentic dishes of their heritage.

Simple is not a word most would use to describe Mexican food. I've heard cheesy, heavy, and even saucy. But never simple. When I started writing this book, I would ask friends and family what came to mind when they thought about Mexican food. Their responses always included baskets of chips and salsa and plates overflowing with rice, refried beans, and sour cream. Definitely not simple. And definitely not Mexican.

Unlike its Tex-Mex cousin, Mexican food is simply built around a few fresh ingredients—primarily tomatoes, chiles, cilantro, and corn—and a small number of basic cooking techniques—mostly roasting, grilling, and stewing. The flavors are clean and vibrant, not masked and muddled.

What is not so simple is Mexico's rich culinary history that dates back hundreds of years. Traditions and flavors are deeply rooted, and there are many recipes that require multiple ingredients, several of which are often handled individually. I will not be addressing those recipes in this book. Instead I've focused on the popular yet practical recipes that can be prepared as a simple weekday dinner for two or for a large weekend gathering for family and friends. After all, what is better than coming home to a warm bowl of homemade tortilla soup or spending a weekend afternoon with friends sipping margaritas and sharing platters of fish tacos, chile-smothered ribs, and charred corn?

Feel confident in knowing that these recipes have been developed with one eye on authenticity and the other on practicality. As a teacher, I want to encourage my students to cook and make the recipes—not discourage them by putting up roadblocks that make cooking unnecessarily complicated. To that end, each recipe includes a section entitled "Cooking Notes," in which I write about ingredients and techniques, and give tips on preparing items in advance and storing them for future use. These are questions that always come up at my classes, and the notes are my way of coaching you while you are cooking.

Sourcing ingredients is one of the biggest recipe deal-breakers. I have found that home cooks will usually try to find ingredients at two markets before giving up on a recipe or finding a suitable substitute, which could mean just eliminating the ingredient from the recipe altogether. While that may be necessary at times, it also does not do the recipe justice. Achiote chicken roasted in aluminum foil is just not the same as when properly roasted in banana leaves. I have tried to offer suitable substitutes for those times when you don't have the real ingredient on hand, but I have also made sure to include those "hard-to-find" ingredients in several recipes so you have plenty of options for using them once you've found them. Nothing is more frustrating than buying a hard-to-find spice just to use $1/2$ teaspoon and never open the jar again! So you will see banana leaves, chipotles, dried ancho chiles, and queso fresco used often throughout the book.

One piece of advice: Read a recipe in its entirety before you start to cook! If I had a dollar for each student I have had who just dives into a recipe, well.... Think of a recipe as a map. If you want to get from point A to point B, you need to understand what is required of you along the way. Otherwise, you will get lost. However, once you've successfully gotten to your destination, getting there a second and third time becomes easier and faster. The same is true with a recipe. The first time you make chicken tamales, the process will seem a bit awkward. But after that, it's smooth sailing. To help you along, I have divided the recipe instructions into distinct steps, each with a highlighted brief summary at its start. Think of these steps as future shortcuts.

I hope you enjoy cooking and learning from this book as much as I have enjoyed writing it. And I hope you realize that cooking—at its core–really is simple!

PANTRY ITEMS

8 ESSENTIAL PRODUCE ITEMS
(items you should always pick up at the market)

Tomatoes
Cilantro
Jalapeños
Red onions
Garlic
Limes
Corn (fresh or frozen)
Avocados

9 ESSENTIAL MEXICAN PRODUCTS
(items to pick up at a Mexican grocery or order online)

Corn husks
Dried ancho chiles
Frozen banana leaves
Fresh corn tortillas (will keep for 1 month in refrigerator)
Masa harina (cornmeal for tamales)
Canned chipotles
Dulce de leche
*Queso fresco
*Mexican crema

*Perishable, so buy what you know you will use.

10 ESSENTIAL MEXICAN PANTRY ITEMS
(items you always want on hand)

Canned chipotles
Red wine vinegar
Dried black beans
Dried ancho chiles
Corn tortillas
Dried oregano
Bay leaves
Ground cumin
Annatto seeds
White rice

Glossary: 25 Ingredients and Terms You Should Know

ANNATTO SEEDS

Also referred to as achiote seeds, these are the reddish, musky seeds of the annatto tree. The very hard seeds must be ground in a spice grinder or blender because they are difficult to break up by hand. Annato is the main ingredient in *recado*, a spice paste used to flavor and color meats and seafood. Annatto comes in both seed and powder form. Avoid the powder because its flavor is not as intense or fresh as the seeds, and the color seems a bit artificial.

ADOBO SAUCE

Ground chiles, usually ancho chiles, make up the base for this sauce, which can be made from scratch or purchased in a can. This spicy sauce is used as a marinade or condiment in many recipes. Chipotle chiles are traditionally canned in adobo sauce.

ANCHO CHILE

This dried brown chile turns a deep red color when rehydrated. It is sweet in flavor and varies in its heat level. The ancho chile gets its name from its broad width (*ancho* means wide in Spanish). It is called poblano when fresh.

BANANA LEAVES

Usually found frozen in the United States, these very large and pliable leaves are primarily used to wrap food that is to be roasted or steamed, in order to infuse the food with a distinctive smoky flavor. The leaves have a spine that must be cut off in order to make the leaves flexible before they are cut to their desired size. They are best kept frozen and can be defrosted and refrozen many times without much consequence. Banana leaves turn a brown color when cooked and are never eaten.

CAYENNE PEPPER

A hot powder made up of finely ground dried cayenne chiles (red peppers).

CEVICHE

Raw fish "cooked" by the acid in citrus fruit, typically lime juice. Although the fish is never heated, its flesh becomes firm and its color becomes opaque. Ceviche is usually served as an appetizer, and the marinade includes chiles, cilantro, and red onion.

CHIPOTLE

A dried, ripe and smoked jalapeño, this chile combines heat with a sweet smoky flavor. Chipotles are dark brown with wrinkled skins and can be found dried or canned. Canned chipotles are packed in adobo sauce.

CHORIZO

Mexican chorizo is a fresh sausage highly flavored with chiles. The casing is typically removed, allowing the meat to impart a rich red color along with a deep slightly spicy flavor.

CILANTRO

The bright green leaves and stems of this fresh herb are ubiquitous in Mexican cooking. Delivering a clean and pungent flavor, the herb is used both raw and cooked. Its tender stems can be used and contribute much flavor. This herb is also known as Chinese parsley.

CORN HUSKS

These dried corn leaves are primarily used for wrapping tamales. They must be reconstituted by submerging in hot water for about 20 minutes. Reconstituted corn husks take on a slightly deeper color. They should be wrapped in a moist towel to maintain their moistness. They are never eaten.

CREMA

While often substituted with sour cream, Mexican crema is much thinner in consistency and richer in flavor. Because crema is a full-fat cream, it can be used in hot foods and recipes without breaking (sour cream is partly made with skim milk and will separate when heated). Pay attention to the label when purchasing the crema because there is both a sour and sweet variety. While it's a matter of taste, the sour variety is the one most often used—and the one I use for the recipes in this book. Sweet crema is not widely available, but it does exist. So, check the label just to make sure you are purchasing the correct product.

DULCE DE LECHE

Similar in taste and appearance to caramel, dulce de leche (sweet milk) is made by slowly heating sweetened milk. Popular throughout Latin America, people in each country have slightly different ways of preparing it. In Mexico, dulce de leche is made solely with cow's milk or with equal proportions of cow and goat milk, in which case it is referred to as *cajeta*.

ENCHILADAS

Enchiladas are corn tortillas stuffed with meat or cheese and smothered with a red tomato or green tomatillo sauce. The stuffed tortillas are then topped with shredded cheese and are typically baked.

JALAPEÑOS

Widely used and available in the United States, these smooth green chiles vary in the heat they give off, which is mostly found in its veins and seeds. Ripened jalapeños are red in color and smoked jalapeños are called chipotles. Canned jalapeños lose their vibrant color and fresh flavor and should be not be used.

JICAMA

A root vegetable with a cream-colored flesh and very thin but inedible skin. The flesh has a slightly sweet, nutty flavor with a crunchy texture; it is often compared to a water chestnut. Jicama is typically served raw but can be boiled, sautéed, or fried. When purchasing, avoid a jicama with a wrinkled skin, which means it is dehydrated and will not have the desired crunchy texture.

MASA

Spanish for dough. In Mexican cooking, *masa* (also called fresh masa) is the term given to the dough used to make tamales, tortillas, and other corn-based products. It is made from dried corn kernels that have been cooked and then soaked in limewater. The wet corn is then ground into a dough. Fresh masa is not easily found in the United States.

MASA HARINA

A commercially manufactured flour made from dried corn kernels that have been treated to make masa, then further ground and dried to make a flour. Maseca is a very popular brand of masa harina sold in the United States.

MEXICAN OREGANO

This oregano has a stronger flavor than the Mediterranean variety, and is typically found in dried form. When purchasing oregano, assume you're getting the Mediterranean variety unless the label specifies the type. I used Mexican oregano when I developed the recipes in this book, but Mediterranean oregano and Mexican oregano can be used interchangeably in these recipes. The selection depends on personal preference and which type you have on hand.

MOLE

One of Mexico's most famous sauces, there are hundreds of variations that originate from one of seven master moles. A common characteristic of a mole is the long list of aromatic ingredients that blend to make the sauce. In the United States, chocolate is probably the most infamous ingredient, but, in fact, not all moles contain chocolate.

POBLANO CHILES

These dark green chiles measure up to 5 inches in length and have an intense flavor with very mild heat. Poblanos are never eaten raw and are usually roasted and peeled. Roasted poblanos sliced into strips are referred to as *rajas*, a term that also applies to other roasted and sliced chiles. Dried poblanos are called ancho chiles.

PEPITAS

Pumpkin seeds that have had their white hull removed. They are best roasted with a bit of salt.

QUESO FRESCO

A fresh cow's milk cheese that is similar in texture to farmer's cheese, queso fresco is slightly salty. It is usually packed in liquid-filled containers to help keep it moist. This is a crumbly cheese that does not melt well.

TAMAL

A prepared masa (cornmeal dough) that is typically stuffed with meat, cheese, or chiles and wrapped in corn husks or banana leaves. Tamales are steamed and unwrapped before being eaten and are often accompanied by crema. While tamales are usually savory snacks, sweet tamales made with milk, nuts, and dried fruit are also served.

TAMAL DOUGH

A dough made by combining masa harina and a liquid, such as chicken broth. It is very commonly used as a substitute for fresh masa.

TOMATILLOS

A fruit enclosed in a papery thin husk, it is often mistakenly called a green tomato. It is not related to the tomato, but rather is part of the gooseberry family and has a fresh tart taste. Tomatillos vary in size, although most are about $2^1/_2$ inches in diameter. When the papery husk is peeled off, tomatillos tend to have a sticky coating that is easily cleaned off with a rinse of water. Tomatillos can be eaten raw or cooked and are available canned. Try to avoid using the canned tomatillos because the color and flavor are inferior.

Appetizers

Crab Tostadas

I often wonder if tostadas—crisp tortillas mounded with your choice of topping—were the first version of modern-day nachos. If so, these would definitely be called "supreme." Crunchy tortillas are layered with slices of creamy avocado and topped with a zesty crab salad to make the perfect appetizer. **SERVES 8**

COOKING NOTES

INGREDIENTS

Tostadas

You can buy commercial tostada shells or fry your own. Commerical tostada shells are basically large tortilla chips. Buy your favorite brand, but try to find tostadas that are 6 to 9 inches wide, round, and flat.

TECHNIQUES

Homemade Tostadas

To make homemade tostadas, purchase 6-inch corn tortillas. Pour 2 inches of oil into a shallow pan and heat over medium-high heat. When the oil is hot, add the tortillas, one at a time, and fry until golden brown on both sides. Remove from the pan, place on a paper towel–lined dish, and sprinkle with salt.

Seeding Tomatoes

To seed tomatoes, cut the tomato into quarters lengthwise then slice off the seedy pulp. Plum tomatoes are best for this recipe because they contain fewer seeds and less pulp than the round varieties.

ADVANCE PREPARATION

The crabmeat mixture can be made a day in advance and refrigerated in an airtight container.

SERVING SUGGESTIONS

While these tostadas make a great first course, you can also make smaller, bite-size ones to be served as hors d'oeuvres.

Another more casual option is to put the crabmeat mixture in a bowl or platter and serve the tortillas alongside, allowing your guests to make their own tostadas. In this case, dice the avocado and fold it into the crabmeat mixture.

1 pound lump crabmeat

1 tablespoon olive oil

2 tablespoons mayonnaise

3 tablespoons finely chopped red onion

1 jalapeño, stemmed and finely chopped

3 plum tomatoes, cored, seeded, and chopped

1/4 cup lightly packed cilantro leaves, chopped

2 limes, finely grated zest and juice

Salt and black pepper

8 flat tostada shells, packaged or homemade

1 avocado, pitted and thinly sliced (see Cooking Notes, page 73)

GARNISH

Cilantro sprigs

2 limes, quartered

PREPARE THE CRABMEAT

Put the crabmeat in a bowl. Pick through it with your fingers to remove any cartilage.

COMBINE THE INGREDIENTS

Add the oil, mayonnaise, onion, jalapeño, tomatoes, cilantro, and lime zest and juice to the crabmeat. Using a rubber spatula or spoon, gently fold (or toss) all ingredients until well blended. Season well with salt and pepper.

ASSEMBLE AND SERVE

Top each tostada shell with a few slices of avocado, place a generous serving of the crabmeat mixture over it, and garnish with a sprig of cilantro. Serve each with a lime wedge.

Fish Ceviche

While ceviche has become increasingly popular in the United States, it has been a staple in the Mexican kitchen for decades. Traditionally fresh fish is "cooked" by the acid of lime juice and flavored with red onion, jalapeño, and cilantro. Ceviche makes a fresh and light start to any meal. This is a good basic ceviche recipe, but feel free to make it your own by adding other aromatic ingredients, such as fresh ginger or tomato. **SERVES 4**

1 pound firm white fish fillet (such as snapper, mahi mahi, sea bass, or tilapia), cut into ¼-inch cubes

¼ red onion, thinly sliced

1 jalapeño, stemmed, seeded (optional), and finely chopped

1 cup lime juice (about 14 limes)

1 teaspoon salt, plus more as needed

1 avocado, pitted and chopped

1 cup lightly packed cilantro leaves, chopped, plus sprigs of cilantro for garnish

Tortilla chips

COOKING NOTES

TECHNIQUES

Chopping an Avocado

The easiest way to chop an avocado is in its skin. But first you have to slice it in half. Cut the avocado in half by slicing halfway into it with a large knife and once you hit the seed in the center, move your knife along its perimeter. Twist the avocado open by gently pulling on each half.

Remove the seed by tapping the seed with the sharp edge of your knife, causing the knife to become wedged into the seed. Twist the knife a bit to dislodge the seed.

Finally, chop the avocado by taking the tip of your knife and drawing a grid onto the avocado flesh. Keep in mind that the tighter the grid, the smaller the dice. Make sure the tip of the knife reaches the skin of the avocado. Use a spoon to scoop out the chopped avocado.

ADVANCE PREPARATION

The ceviche is best eaten the day it is made, but you can hold it for up to 2 days in the refrigerator. For best results, keep the ceviche wrapped under the two layers of plastic wrap.

MARINATE THE FISH

Combine the fish, onion, and jalapeño in a nonreactive (ceramic, glass, or plastic) bowl and pour in the lime juice. Make sure all of the fish is covered in juice.

Take a piece of plastic wrap large enough to cover the entire surface of the dish and press onto the fish mixture to create a plastic barrier between the fish and the air. Next, cover the entire bowl with a second layer of plastic wrap and refrigerate for at least 3 hours or up to 8 hours.

SEASON THE CEVICHE

Season the ceviche with the salt and stir well. Cover again with both layers of plastic wrap and return to the refrigerator for another hour.

ADD THE AVOCADO AND CILANTRO

Mix in the avocado and cilantro. Taste and adjust the seasoning if needed.

GARNISH AND SERVE

Serve the ceviche on a large platter or in individual dishes. Top the dish with sprigs of cilantro and accompany with tortilla chips.

Chicken Quesadillas

Quesadilla literally translates to "little cheese thing." In Mexico, these little cheese turnovers are eaten as snacks throughout the day and can be left plain or stuffed with a filling. The filling is a combination of regional and personal preference. In all cases, these portable turnovers are quick and easy to make with ingredients you are most likely to have on hand—making them the perfect snack! **SERVES 6**

1 onion, halved

2 cloves garlic, crushed

$1/2$ teaspoon salt

5 cups water

$3/4$ pound (1 large or 2 small) skinless, boneless chicken breasts

2 bay leaves

1 teaspoon dried oregano

6 fresh corn tortillas

$1^1/2$ cups (6 ounces) shredded Monterey Jack cheese

2 to 3 tablespoons olive oil

1 cup Fresh Tomato Salsa (page 96)

1 cup Mexican crema, homemade (page 102) or store-bought

COOKING NOTES

INGREDIENTS

Fillings for Quesadillas

Omitting the chicken from this recipe will give you a classic cheese quesadilla. Using this as a base, you can create plain quesadillas or stuff them with whatever filling you choose: cooked chorizo (page 71), sautéed zucchini, etc.

TECHNIQUES

Heating Quesadillas

Quesadillas should have a slightly crispy texture, which is only achieved by searing them with a bit of oil. If you plan to grill them, brush the outside of the tortilla with oil to achieve the crispy exterior.

ADVANCE PREPARATION

Quesadillas are best eaten just after being made, but if you want to make them ahead of time, you can keep them, covered, in a warm oven (200°F) for up to 1 hour.

POACH AND SHRED THE CHICKEN

Combine the onion, garlic, salt, and water in a saucepan and bring to a boil. Add the chicken, bay leaves, and oregano and lower the heat to a simmer. Cook the chicken, partially covered, for 35 minutes.

Check for doneness. Since you are going to shred the chicken anyway, slit the chicken in half to make sure the inside is cooked through. The chicken is ready when its interior is no longer pink in color and the juices run clear.

Allow the chicken to cool in the broth. When cool enough to handle, remove the chicken from the pan and, if desired, reserve the broth for future use. Shred the chicken by hand by pulling apart its fibers with your fingers and set aside.

ASSEMBLE THE QUESADILLAS

Place a tortilla in front of you and sprinkle 2 tablespoons cheese on the bottom half. Top with 2 tablespoons shredded chicken and another 2 tablespoons cheese. Fold the tortilla over creating a half circle. Repeat with the remaining tortillas (they may not stay closed—but don't worry about it).

HEAT THE QUESADILLAS

Place a large skillet over high heat and add 1 tablespoon of the olive oil. When the oil is hot, place an assembled quesadilla (in its half circle shape) in the pan, making sure to hold down the top until the cheese begins to melt, creating a glue to hold the tortilla in place. Add as many quesadillas as you can comfortably fit in the pan.

After a couple of minutes, flip the quesadillas over and heat the other side for another 2 minutes. Remove from the pan and repeat with the remaining quesadillas, adding more oil as needed.

GARNISH AND SERVE

You can leave the quesadillas whole or cut them in half to serve. Place the quesadillas on a platter and serve with fresh tomato salsa and Mexican crema.

Chile, Cheese & Chorizo Melt

Talk about a crowd-pleaser. This version of a *fundido*—a Mexican fondue—is incredibly addicting. I challenge you to walk away from this melted gooey cheese mixed with meaty chorizo and spicy poblano chile strips. It is impossible! **SERVES 6 TO 8**

2 poblano chiles

1 tablespoon olive oil

1 cup (8 ounces) Mexican chorizo, homemade (page 71) or store-bought, casing removed

4 cups (16 ounces) shredded or cubed Monterey Jack cheese

Tortilla chips

COOKING NOTES
INGREDIENTS

Poblano Chiles

What these mild chiles lack in heat, they make up for in flavor. If you cannot find them, you can substitute 1 roasted jalapeño chile. Just be careful—since the jalapeño is a spicy chile, you want to make sure to finely chop it so its heat will be well distributed in the dish.

ADVANCE PREPARATION

Although you need to serve this dish as soon as the bubbly cheese is broiled, you can prepare this recipe in advance to the point where you cover the baking dish with foil. It can be held at this stage for a few hours in the refrigerator. Make sure to bring it to room temperature before baking.

SERVING SUGGESTION

Divide the cheese mixture into small ramekins and make individual servings that you can place on a dinner plate as an unexpected side dish.

ROAST AND PREPARE POBLANOS

Over an open flame of a gas stove or barbeque grill or in a dry cast-iron or nonstick skillet over high heat, roast the chiles until they are charred on all sides. This will take a few minutes over an open flame and about 10 minutes in a skillet.

Remove the chiles from the heat and seal in a plastic bag for 5 minutes. This will create steam and allow the skins to separate from the flesh. If you don't have a plastic bag, place the chiles in a bowl and cover tightly with aluminum foil or plastic wrap.

Peel away the skins. Cut off the stem end and remove the seeds and veins from the interior. Slice lenghtwise into 1/2-inch-wide strips.

PREHEAT THE OVEN

Preheat the oven to 350°F.

SAUTÉ THE CHORIZO

Pour the oil into a sauté pan and place the pan over medium-high heat. When the oil is hot, add the chorizo. Break up the meat and sauté until the meat browns and develops a slight crust.

BAKE AND BROIL THE CHEESE MIXTURE

Combine the roasted poblano strips and sautéed chorizo in a 1 1/2-quart ovenproof dish. (The dish can be any shape but should hold all of the ingredients, including the cheese, comfortably.) Toss well. Add the cheese and toss again, making sure to evenly distribute the chorizo and poblano strips.

Cover the dish with aluminum foil and bake for 20 minutes. Remove the foil and broil the dish for about 3 minutes, or until the cheese begins to bubble.

SERVE

Serve immediately with tortilla chips.

Chiles Stuffed with Corn & Crema

Stuffed chiles—a.k.a. chiles rellenos—are only as good as their stuffing. These are made with corn, cheese, and crema, combining sweet and salty with some mild heat. But dare to experiment by adding mushrooms, ground meat, or chorizo to the filling for a heartier version. This eye-catching appetizer also makes for a great side dish. **SERVES 6**

COOKING NOTES
INGREDIENTS

Poblano Chiles

There really is no substitute for the rich-tasting and slightly hot poblano chile. Resist using a bell pepper in its place because the flavor and color of the dish will not be the same.

Frozen Corn

If you are using frozen corn, measure the amount needed before defrosting.

Mexican Crema

Do not substitute sour cream for the crema in this recipe because sour cream tends to separate when baked. A suitable substitute would be crème fraîche.

TECHNIQUE

Removing Corn Kernels

I find that the easiest way to do this is to work with the corn in a horizontal position and essentially slice four sides off of the ear of corn. You will need a large chef's knife. Place the corn on a cutting board lengthwise in front of you and position the tip of your knife blade on the top right side of the corn then slice off the entire right side. To help avoid cutting into the cob, place your blade one kernel in from the edge. Rotate the ear of corn clockwise and repeat with the remaining three sides.

ADVANCE PREPARATION

The chiles can be roasted a day in advance and kept covered in the refrigerator. The corn mixture also can be sautéed ahead of time. The chiles can be assembled a few hours in advance, but should be baked just before serving.

6 poblano chiles

Kernels from 5 ears fresh corn, or 3 cups frozen corn, defrosted

2 tablespoons olive oil

1 red onion, chopped

2 cloves garlic, finely chopped

$1/2$ teaspoon salt, plus more as needed

Black pepper

2 cups (8 ounces) shredded Monterey Jack cheese

$1/2$ cup Mexican crema, homemade (page 102) or store-bought

ROAST AND PREPARE THE POBLANOS

Over an open flame of a gas stove or barbeque grill or in a dry cast-iron or nonstick skillet over high heat, roast the chiles until they are charred on all sides. This will take a few minutes over an open flame and about 10 minutes in a skillet.

Remove the chiles from the heat and seal in a plastic bag for 5 minutes. This will create steam and allow the skins to separate from the flesh. If you don't have a plastic bag, place the chiles in a bowl and cover tightly with aluminum foil or plastic wrap.

Peel away the skins. Cut a slit down one side of each roasted and peeled poblano chile, starting just under the stem and going all the way down to the tip. Remove all the seeds and as much of the veins as you can, being careful not to rip the chile. Set aside.

SAUTÉ THE CORN MIXTURE

If you are using fresh corn, husk the corn, remove the silks, and slice the kernels from the cobs with a knife. Pour the oil into a large sauté pan set over medium-high heat. When the oil is hot, add the onion and garlic and sauté until the onion becomes translucent, about 2 minutes. Add the corn kernels, season with the salt and pepper, and continue cooking for 5 minutes, or until the corn begins to just turn a golden brown color. Set aside.

STUFF, BAKE, AND BROIL THE POBLANOS

Preheat the oven to 375°F.

Stuff $^1/_2$ cup of the sautéed corn mixture into a chile. Top the corn with $^1/_4$ cup shredded cheese, $1^1/_2$ tablespoons crema, and another $1^1/_2$ tablespoons shredded cheese. The chile should be fat and full. Place the stuffed chile, slit side up, in a baking dish and repeat with the remaining chiles. (The size and shape of the baking dish is not important, as long as the chiles are placed in a single layer.) Arrange the chiles side by side in the dish; they can be touching, if needed. It's a good idea to select a dish that you would be happy taking to the table, as the chiles are best eaten straight from the oven.

Bake for 10 minutes. Then broil for 5 minutes, or until the cheese turns golden brown and bubbly.

SERVE

Serve warm in the baking dish or transfer to a serving platter.

Mexican Bar Snacks:
Chile & Lime Jicama Wedges, Toasted Pumpkin Seeds, Chile-Spiced Peanuts

Snacking is as much a Mexican pastime as it is an American one. These snacks, which are sold by street vendors, go great with beer and cocktails. Served as a trio or on their own, they are incredibly addicting! **MAKES 1 CUPFUL OF EACH**

COOKING NOTES
INGREDIENTS

Cayenne Pepper

While you can use almost any type of dried chile powder for these recipes, I like cayenne for both its heat and availability. Ancho chile powder would be a good mild substitute. Just be careful with blended dried chile mixes, such as generic chili powder, because they are blends of garlic, oregano, and other spices.

TECHNIQUES

Julienned Lime Zest

The easiest way to julienne lime zest is with a citrus zester. If you do not have a zester, you can finely grate the zest with a box grater or a rasp.

Melting Sugar

Melting sugar is not difficult so long as you use the proper tools. For this you will need two items—a nonstick pan and a heatproof silicone spatula. Equipment of any other material will cause the melted sugar mixture to stick to it, making it difficult to handle, and the equipment will seem impossible to clean.

ADVANCE PREPARATION

The pumpkin seeds and peanuts can be made well in advance—up to 24 hours before you are going to serve. Both should be kept in airtight containers at room temperature.

The jicama should be made no more than 4 hours in advance. Keep it in the refrigerator and mix in the cayenne pepper 30 minutes before serving.

CHILE & LIME JICAMA WEDGES
1 small jicama (about 4 inches in diameter)
1 lime, finely julienned zest and juice
$1/8$ teaspoon cayenne pepper, or to taste
$1/4$ teaspoon salt, or to taste

To prepare the jicama, trim the peel from the jicama with a sharp knife. Cut the jicama into $1/4$-inch strips or wedges and put into a bowl. Toss in the lime zest, lime juice, cayenne, and salt and mix well. Serve.

TOASTED PUMPKIN SEEDS
1 tablespoon olive oil
1 cup shelled pumpkin seeds
$1/2$ teaspoon salt

To toast the seeds, heat the oil in a nonstick pan over medium-high heat. When the oil is hot, add the pumpkin seeds. Toss well in the oil and sprinkle in the salt. Toast for 2 to 3 minutes, until the pumpkin seeds begin to pop and release their fragrance. Transfer to a small bowl and serve.

CHILE-SPICED PEANUTS
1 cup roasted, unsalted peanuts
3 tablespoons sugar
1 teaspoon cayenne pepper
1 teaspoon coarse salt
1 lime, quartered

To toast the peanuts, heat a nonstick pan over high heat. Add the peanuts and shake the pan often so that the nuts do not burn but rather toast slightly. After about 2 minutes you should begin to smell the aroma of toasted nuts. Remove the nuts from the pan and set aside.

To make the spice mixture, decrease the heat to medium and return the pan to the stove. Sprinkle in the sugar, cayenne, and coarse salt (be careful because the heated cayenne can cause coughing).

Allow the mixture to melt slowly, stirring lightly with a heatproof silicone spatula. As soon as all the sugar has melted, return the peanuts to the pan and coat well with the sugar mixture. The peanut mixture may clump a bit, but that is okay.

Invert the spiced nuts onto a sheet of parchment paper. Allow the nuts to cool and the sugar to set for a few minutes.

Serve with wedges of lime for guests to squeeze over their nuts right before eating.

Soups & Salads

Tortilla Soup • 20

Fresh Corn Soup Topped with
Roasted Corn Guacamole • 22

Shredded Cabbage & Radish Slaw • 24

Tangy Jicama Salad • 25

Chipotle-Glazed Steak & Avocado Salad • 26

Chilled Shrimp & Lime Salad • 29

Creamy Chicken Chipotle Salad • 30

Watercress Salad with Cilantro Dressing • 31

Tortilla Soup

If there is a recipe that truly captures the scent and essence of Mexican cooking, this is it. There are so many reasons to love this soup. Besides being easy to make and healthful to eat, it offers deep, rich flavors brightened by fresh ingredients. This is a great soup to serve for company, because it is not only delicious, but the contrasting colors of the deep amber soup base and the bright green and white from the toppings make for a stunning presentation. It is also a conversation piece, because everyone can get involved in the assembly of their soup bowl. **SERVES 6**

COOKING NOTES
INGREDIENTS

Corn Tortillas for Frying

You will get better results if you use dried-out tortillas. If you remember, leave your tortillas out and uncovered on the counter for a few hours.

TECHNIQUES

Frying Tortilla Strips

Do not shy away from frying your own tortilla strips. While you can simply purchase commercial tostada shells and break them up, you will be sacrificing flavor, texture, and a beautiful presentation.

I am not a big proponent of frying indoors, but this method is really just shallow-frying. And if you use olive oil, it will not cause you or your house to smell like the inside of a fryolator.

Work in batches if your pan is not large enough to accommodate the tortilla strips in a single layer. After frying in 1-inch deep oil, make sure you drain the strips on a paper towel and sprinkle immediately with salt. This will guarantee that the salt adheres to the tortillas.

COOKING NOTES
TECHNIQUES

Chopping an Avocado

The easiest way to chop an avocado is in its skin. But first you have to slice it in half. Cut the avocado in half by slicing halfway into it with a large knife and once you hit the seed in the center, move your knife along its perimeter. Twist the avocado open by gently pulling on each half.

Remove the seed by tapping the seed with the sharp edge of your knife, causing the knife to become wedged into the seed. Twist the knife a bit to dislodge the seed.

Finally, chop the avocado by taking the tip of your knife and drawing a grid onto the avocado flesh. Keep in mind that the tighter the grid, the smaller the dice. Make sure the tip of the knife reaches the skin of the avocado. Use a spoon to scoop out the chopped avocado.

ADVANCE PREPARATION

Not only can everything for this recipe be prepared in advance, the flavor of the broth is actually better after sitting in the refrigerator for a day. The tortillas also can be fried a day or two in advance and kept in an airtight container, such as a sealable plastic bag.

The avocado and cilantro can be prepared 30 minutes before serving.

SOUP BASE

2 large tomatoes

1 onion, peeled

3 cloves garlic, not peeled

2 tablespoons olive oil

6 cups chicken broth

Salt

SOUP TOPPINGS

Olive oil for frying tortillas

4 fresh corn tortillas, cut into thin strips

Salt

1 avocado, pitted and chopped

$1/2$ cup Mexican crema, homemade (page 102) or
    store-bought

$1/2$ cup queso fresco or feta cheese, crumbled

$1/4$ cup lightly packed fresh cilantro leaves

2 limes, quartered

ROAST AND PUREE THE VEGETABLES
FOR THE SOUP BASE

Put the tomatoes, onion, and garlic in a dry cast-iron or nonstick skillet over medium-high heat. Allow the vegetables to roast and char on all sides by rotating them and turning them over with a pair of tongs every few minutes or so. This should take approximately 10 minutes. When all sides are charred, remove the vegetables from the heat and allow to cool slightly. Peel off the blistered skin of the garlic.

Put the toasted vegetables in a blender and puree until smooth.

FRY THE VEGETABLE PUREE AND SIMMER THE SOUP

Heat 2 tablespoons oil in a soup pot over medium-high heat. When the oil is hot, add the roasted vegetable puree. It should sizzle and splatter a bit. Cook the puree, stirring often, until the mixture reduces by half and darkens, 6 to 8 minutes.

Season the reduced puree with 2 teaspoons salt and add the broth. Stir to combine well, bring to a boil, and then decrease the heat to a simmer. Continue simmering, uncovered, for 20 minutes. Taste for seasoning and adjust if needed.

FRY THE TORTILLAS STRIPS

Pour 1 inch of oil into a pan. Place the pan over high heat and wait for the oil to get hot (you can test it by dipping a tortilla strip in the oil—if it sizzles, it is ready). Add the tortilla strips to the hot oil and use a pair of tongs to distribute well. They will take about 5 minutes to become crispy and golden brown. During that time, move them around to make sure they are cooking evenly.

When the tortilla strips become golden brown, remove them from the oil, drain on a paper towel, and sprinkle with salt. Set aside.

ASSEMBLE AND SERVE THE SOUP

Put the avocado, crema, queso fresco, and cilantro in individual small bowls at the table. Serve the soup in bowls and squeeze a wedge of lime into each one. Allow your guests to garnish their soup bowls with the toppings of their choice. This method not only makes for a beautiful presentation, it also keeps the toppings fresh.

Fresh Corn Soup Topped with Roasted Corn Guacamole

I really love this soup. The flavors will remind you of corn chowder, but the texture is much lighter. The soup is bright and fresh and can be made year-round since it tastes just as good when using frozen corn as it does when using fresh. **SERVES 4 TO 6**

COOKING NOTES

INGREDIENTS

Frozen corn

If you are using frozen corn, measure the amount needed before defrosting.

TECHNIQUE

Removing Corn Kernels

I find that the easiest way to do this is to work with the corn in a horizontal position and essentially slice four sides off of the ear of corn. You will need a large chef's knife. Place the corn on a cutting board lengthwise in front of you and position the tip of your knife blade on the top right side of the corn then slice off the entire right side. To help avoid cutting into the cob, place your blade one kernel in from the edge. Rotate the ear of corn clockwise and repeat with the remaining three sides.

Roasting Corn

Roasting corn not only caramelizes the naturally present sugars, it also intensifies the flavor of the corn. Twenty minutes is the average time it takes to get the corn to that state, but don't be afraid to leave it in a bit longer. Even if some kernels appear burnt, they will be deliciously crunchy and pop in your mouth.

ADVANCE PREPARATION

The soup can be made a day in advance, cooled, and stored in the refrigerator. However, it is best to make the corn guacamole a few hours before you are going to eat it.

ROASTED CORN GUACAMOLE

Kernels from 3 ears fresh corn, or 2 cups frozen corn, defrosted
1 tablespoon olive oil
Salt and black pepper
1 tablespoon finely chopped red onion
2 tablespoons fresh cilantro, finely chopped
1 lime, finely grated zest and juice
1 jalapeño, stemmed and seeded, finely chopped
1 avocado, pitted and chopped (see Cooking Notes, page 20)

SOUP

Kernels from 5 ears fresh corn, or 3 cups frozen corn, defrosted
2 tablespoons olive oil
1 clove garlic, crushed
1/2 red onion, chopped
1 jalapeño, stemmed and chopped
Salt and black pepper
1 1/2 cups chicken broth
Cilantro sprigs, to garnish

ROAST THE CORN FOR THE GUACAMOLE

Preheat the oven to 450°F. Prepare a baking sheet by lining it with parchment paper or aluminum foil.

Put the corn kernels on the baking sheet and toss with the oil, 1/4 teaspoon salt, and black pepper to taste. Spread the corn out evenly on the baking sheet and roast for 20 minutes, until the corn turns a golden brown. It may seem that you have left the corn in the oven for too long, but you want the corn to caramelize and get a little crunchy. Remove the corn from the oven and set aside.

PREPARE THE CORN FOR THE SOUP

Put the kernels (fresh or frozen and defrosted) in a blender.

Combine the oil and the garlic in a soup pot over medium heat. Add the onion and jalapeño. Season with salt and pepper and sauté until the vegetables are soft and translucent, about 6 minutes. Transfer the vegetables to the blender and puree until smooth. (You may need to pulse or stir the corn mixture in order to achieve a smooth consistency, but do not add any more liquid.)

SIMMER THE SOUP

Pour the corn puree into the soup pot and place over medium heat. Stir constantly for a few minutes, until the soup begins to thicken. Slowly whisk or stir in the chicken broth. Bring to a boil, decrease the heat to a simmer, cover, and cook for 15 minutes.

FINISH THE ROASTED CORN GUACAMOLE

In a bowl, combine the roasted corn, red onion, cilantro, lime zest and juice, and jalapeño. Gently stir in the avocado. Season with salt and pepper.

SERVE AND GARNISH

Ladle the soup into soup bowls. Place a generous spoonful of the guacamole in the center of each bowl. Garnish with a small sprig of cilantro placed in the center of each.

Shredded Cabbage & Radish Slaw

Mexican taco stands typically offer crunchy pickled vegetables to accompany their tacos. Shredded cabbage and sliced radishes are often found in small containers marinating in vinegar, to which guests can help themselves. The contrasting colors and textures, along with the vivid flavors of these toppings, make for a great salad and accompaniment to any meal. **SERVES 6**

COOKING NOTES
TECHNIQUES

Shredding Cabbage

The slicing side of a box grater works really well for this. However, if you don't have one, you can shred the cabbage with your knife by cutting the cabbage in half, removing its core, and then slicing the cabbage very thinly.

Marinating the Vegetables

I find marinating vegetables in a sealed plastic bag that has had all of its air expelled is an efficient way of making sure all the vegetables have been exposed to the marinade. (It is also compact enough to fit easily in your refrigerator.) If you don't have a plastic bag, use whatever container you have on hand. In that case, just make sure to stir the vegetables often.

ADVANCE PREPARATION

The vegetables can marinate overnight and will benefit from the extra time. However, in order for the cilantro to stay fresh, toss it with the olive oil no sooner than 1 hour before serving.

^{1}/$_2$ small head white cabbage, cored and
    thinly shredded (3 cups)

3 large radishes, sliced into thin strips (^{1}/$_2$ cup)

2 scallions, tops trimmed and thinly sliced (^{1}/$_4$ cup)

^{1}/$_2$ cup red wine vinegar

1 teaspoon salt

1 teaspoon sugar

1^1/$_2$ tablespoons olive oil

2 tablespoons fresh cilantro leaves, chopped,
    plus 1 sprig for garnish

Black pepper

MARINATE THE VEGETABLES

Combine the cabbage, radishes, scallions, vinegar, salt, and sugar in a sealable plastic bag and mix well. Expel as much air as possible and seal the bag. Allow the vegetables to marinate for at least 30 minutes, and up to overnight.

REMOVE THE SALAD FROM THE MARINATING LIQUID

Using tongs or two forks, remove the vegetables from the marinating liquid (allow excess vinegar to drain off) and place in a mixing bowl. Discard the remaining vinegar mixture.

FINISH THE SALAD AND SERVE

Before serving, add the olive oil, cilantro, and black pepper and toss well. Check for seasoning and adjust if necessary.

Transfer to a serving dish and garnish with a fresh sprig of cilantro.

Tangy Jicama Salad

This salad is as crunchy as it is tangy, which makes it the perfect refreshing complement to any Mexican dish. While the salad is very flavorful, it is not overpowering and can offer freshness and texture to a menu. Feel free to omit the cucumber or substitute radish, carrot, or any other hearty vegetable that won't wilt after being left to marinate in lime juice. **SERVES 6**

1 pound jicama (about 5 inches wide), peeled and cut into thin strips

1 English (seedless) cucumber, cut in half lengthwise and sliced vertically into thin strips

3 limes

$1/2$ cup lightly packed fresh cilantro leaves, plus sprigs for garnish

$1/2$ teaspoon salt, plus more as needed

Cayenne pepper

COMBINE THE VEGETABLES

Toss the jicama and cucumber in a large bowl. Juice two of the limes. Add the lime juice, cilantro leaves, and salt and allow to marinate, covered, for 30 minutes at room temperature or in the refrigerator.

SEASON, GARNISH, AND SERVE

Right before serving, sprinkle with the cayenne and taste for seasoning. Add more salt, if necessary and toss.

Transfer the salad to a serving bowl. Cut the remaining lime into quarters. Garnish the salad with sprigs of fresh cilantro and extra lime wedges.

Chipotle-Glazed Steak and Avocado Salad

I love steak salads. It must be something about the contrast in texture and temperature that I find appealing. The best steak salads give you meat that is juicy and flavorful with a charred exterior crust on the steak that goes great against the fresh, crisp lettuce. The glaze is the key to this salad because the sugars in it caramelize and create that crunchy exterior. **SERVES 4**

1/4 red onion, sliced

Red wine vinegar

1 large (or 2 small) head butter lettuce, torn into bite-size pieces

1 cup cherry tomatoes, quartered

1 avocado, pitted and chopped (see Cooking Notes, page 10)

3 tablespoons olive oil

Salt and black pepper

1/4 cup ketchup

1 tablespoon honey

2 canned chipotle chiles

1 tablespoon adobo sauce from canned chipotles

1 1/2 pounds skirt steak or flank steak

1/4 cup Mexican queso fresco or feta cheese, crumbled

1 tablespoon roasted pumpkin seeds (optional)

COOKING NOTES
INGREDIENTS

Skirt Steak versus Flank Steak

Because they are so flavorful, these cuts are both great choices for the salad. Both are long flat pieces of meat, but the flank steak is much leaner and can dry out easily, so keep your eye on it when grilling.

Because skirt steak is a bit fatty, it may need to be trimmed a bit before cooking.

TECHNIQUES

Glazing Meat

Glazes provide flavor and texture to grilled meat. In order to do so, they must contain sugar so that it caramelizes in the heat and creates a crisp exterior with a depth of flavor. The sugar in this glaze is found in the ketchup and in the honey. And, in the same way that sugars caramelize, they can also burn. Brush glazes (and barbecue sauces) on meat toward the end of the grilling to avoid a burnt, bitter taste.

MARINATE THE ONION

Put the onion in a small bowl and pour in enough red wine vinegar to cover well. Set aside for at least 30 minutes.

PREPARE THE SALAD AND DRESSING

Combine the lettuce, tomatoes, and avocado in a serving bowl or platter.

In a small bowl, whisk together 2 tablespoons of the red wine vinegar from the marinating onion, 2 tablespoons of olive oil, and salt and pepper to taste. Set aside until you are ready to dress the salad.

PREPARE THE GLAZE

Combine the ketchup, honey, chipotles, adobo sauce, and 1 teaspoon salt in a blender and puree. Set aside.

SEASON, GRILL, AND GLAZE THE MEAT

Preheat a grill to medium-high for 10 minutes or preheat a grill pan over medium-high heat. Brush the grill grates or grill pan with the remaining tablespoon of oil.

Season the beef on both sides with salt and pepper. Grill the meat for 4 minutes, turn over, and brush the glaze over the steak. Grill for another 4 minutes, turn over, and glaze the other side. Allow the meat to cook for another 2 minutes on each side to caramelize the glaze.

Remove from heat and allow the meat to rest for 5 minutes before slicing into 1/2-inch-wide strips. (This is for medium-rare beef. If you want your meat cooked longer, increase the time you grill the beef before adding the glaze.)

ASSEMBLE THE SALAD AND SERVE

Pour the dressing over the lettuce mixture and toss well. Place the sliced beef over the salad and top with cheese crumbles, marinated red onions, and roasted pumpkin seeds. Serve.

Chilled Shrimp & Lime Salad

This is a wonderfully refreshing salad that walks the line between a shrimp cocktail and a ceviche. It's also incredibly forgiving—so feel free to use as much (or little) of the ingredients as you like. Tangy and fresh, it is a great start to any meal. **SERVES 6**

COOKING NOTES
TECHNIQUES

Preparing Citrus Fruit Zest

The zest of citrus fruit is the outermost layer of the fruit's skin. It adds an incredible burst of flavor and color to recipes. Use a box grater, rasp, or citrus zester to remove the skin. Make sure to only remove the colored part of the peel; the white pith is a bit bitter.

Butterflying Shrimp

A butterflied shrimp is a shrimp that has been sliced lengthwise. In some cases, one side of the shrimp is kept attached, but other times it is sliced all the way through. For this recipe, the shrimp will be sliced in half all the way through.

Peel and devein the shrimp. Place a shrimp on your cutting board and hold your knife blade along the indentation found along the back of the shrimp (the site of the deveining). Slice the shrimp in half lengthwise using the indentation as your guide.

Preparing the shrimp in this manner before blanching will give the shrimp a nice shape after they have been cooked. It will also allow them to cook and cool quickly, thereby preventing them from becoming rubbery.

ADVANCE PREPARATION

This salad can be prepared several hours ahead of time, which will allow the flavors to blend well. If you are preparing the salad in advance, add the salt and cilantro right before serving. Marinating the salad with the salt will toughen the shrimp and cause the vegetables to go limp. Adding the cilantro at the end will ensure that it keeps its texture and will not become too soggy.

1 pound shrimp, peeled, deveined, and butterflied

1 cup cherry tomatoes, quartered

1 red bell pepper, thinly sliced

$^1/_4$ red onion, thinly sliced (about $^1/_2$ cup)

1 cup lightly packed fresh cilantro leaves, chopped, plus sprigs for garnish

1 jalapeño, stemmed and finely chopped

1 avocado, pitted and chopped (see Cooking Notes, page 10)

1 teaspoon salt, or more to taste

Black pepper

7 limes

1 tablespoon prepared horseradish

1 tablespoon ketchup

2 tablespoons olive oil

Corn nuts, for garnish

BLANCH THE SHRIMP

Bring a pot of salted water to a boil. Meanwhile, prepare an ice bath by filling a bowl with ice and cold water.

Add the shrimp to the boiling water and allow to cook for 1 minute. Remove the shrimp from the pot with a slotted spoon and immediately plunge into the ice bath. Allow the shrimp to cool thoroughly, then drain and place on paper towels to absorb some of the water. Transfer the shrimp to a bowl.

PREPARE THE VEGETABLES

Add the tomatoes, red pepper, onion, cilantro, jalapeño, and avocado to the shrimp. Season with salt and pepper and toss lightly.

PREPARE THE DRESSING

Finely grate the zest of 3 of the limes and juice 6 limes. Combine the zest and juice in a small bowl. Mix in the horseradish, ketchup, and olive oil. Pour this dressing over the shrimp salad and toss well. Check seasoning and adjust if necessary.

GARNISH AND SERVE

Slice the remaining lime into wedges. Transfer the salad to a serving platter and garnish with sprigs of cilantro and lime wedges. Sprinkle corn nuts over the salad for added crunch.

Creamy Chicken Chipotle Salad

This is a great main-course salad that brings together many of the fresh flavors of the Mexican kitchen. Similar in nature to a Cobb salad, it has a few fresh components that can be doubled or substituted, making it a great vehicle for using up extra produce. **SERVES 4 TO 6**

1 pound (about 3) skinless, boneless chicken breasts

Olive oil

Salt and black pepper

1/2 cup Chipotle Chile Sauce (page 94)

1 head bibb lettuce, ripped into small pieces

1 pint cherry tomatoes, quartered

1 avocado, pitted and chopped (see Cooking Notes, page 10)

2 tablespoons cilantro leaves, chopped

2 tablespoons olive oil

2 tablespoons red wine vinegar

COOKING NOTES

INGREDIENTS

Chicken

While the recipe uses grilled chicken breast, feel free to use any type of leftover chicken you have on hand or substitute with store-bought rotisserie chicken.

You may want to make extra chicken because once it's tossed with the chipotle sauce it can be eaten in sandwiches or with crackers.

Vegetarian Option

For a meatless alternative, substitute garbanzo beans for the chicken, tossing the beans with the chipotle sauce and cilantro leaves.

ADVANCE PREPARATION

The chicken can be cooked and tossed with the chipotle sauce a day or two in advance and refrigerated in an airtight container.

GRILL THE CHICKEN

Preheat a grill to medium-high for 10 minutes or preheat a grill pan over medium-high heat. Lightly oil the grates or cooking grid. Season the chicken breasts on both sides with salt and pepper. Grill until cooked through, about 5 minutes on each side. Remove the chicken from the heat and allow to cool.

TOSS THE CHICKEN WITH THE SAUCE

Once the chicken is cool enough to handle, roughly chop it into bite-size chunks and lightly toss it with the chipotle sauce until the chicken is well smothered. You can add as much or as little as you like; you may not use all the sauce. Save any leftover sauce and serve it alongside the salad.

PREPARE THE SALAD

In a large mixing bowl, toss together the lettuce, tomatoes, avocado, and 1 tablespoon of the cilantro leaves. Pour in the oil and vinegar and toss well.

GARNISH AND SERVE

Spoon the salad onto a serving platter and top with the chicken. Garnish by sprinkling the remaining 1 tablespoon cilantro over the chicken. Serve any leftover chipotle sauce in a small bowl on the side.

Watercress Salad with Cilantro Dressing

Watercress is such a hearty and flavorful green that it is best when it stands alone, which is why this is basically a green salad. It is also a great accompaniment to any dish in this book—or any Mexican dish—because it is assertive enough to stand up to bold flavors. And don't think the dressing is to be used just for salads—it makes a great sandwich spread or vegetable dip. **SERVES 4**

1 bunch cilantro, tough stems removed
    (about 2 cups lightly packed)

$1/4$ cup olive oil

3 tablespoons red wine vinegar

$1/4$ teaspoon salt, plus more as needed

1 bunch watercress, tough stems removed
    (about $2^1/_2$ cups packed)

$1/4$ cup queso fresco or feta cheese, or to taste

MAKE THE DRESSING

Combine the cilantro, oil, vinegar, and salt in a blender and puree until smooth. Check for seasoning and adjust if necessary.

DRESS THE SALAD

As soon as you are ready to serve the salad, pour 2 tablespoons of the dressing in a mixing bowl. Add the watercress and toss well. If needed, add more dressing. Keep the extra dressing in the refrigerator for a future use.

Transfer the salad to its serving dish and top with crumbles of queso fresco.

Seafood

Chile-Smothered Shrimp Skewers

If you are looking for an easy and delicious recipe that can feed a crowd, you've found it! What's great about this recipe is that most of the "dirty" work can be done ahead of time, leaving only the actual grilling or sautéing of the shrimp to do right before you are ready to eat. Once you see how enticing the chile-smothered skewers look on a platter garnished with fresh cilantro and lime wedges, I guarantee it will become your go-to dish. And if you are not a fan of shrimp, chicken can be substituted easily. Note: You will need eight 6-inch wooden skewers for this recipe. **SERVES 4**

COOKING NOTES
TECHNIQUES

Soaking Wooden Skewers

In order to prevent the skewers from burning, it's important to soak them in water before they're exposed to heat. Place the skewers in a tall glass and fill with water. Allow them to soak for 10 minutes. If they are not completely submerged, flip the skewers over and soak for another 10 minutes. If you are planning on sautéing, it's best to use 6-inch skewers. Longer ones will be difficult to fit comfortably in a sauté pan.

Marinating the Shrimp

I find that the most efficient—not to mention easiest and most space-saving—way to marinate is by using a plastic freezer bag. Make sure to let out as much air as possible before sealing the bag and placing it in the refrigerator. Freezer bags are best because they are thicker and less likely to get punctured by the skewers.

ADVANCE PREPARATION

The Red Chile Paste can hold almost indefinitely in the refrigerator. The shrimp (or meat of choice) can be left to marinate for up to 24 hours.

SERVING SUGGESTIONS

An alternative recipe is to eliminate the skewers and sauté the marinated shrimp in olive oil. After sautéing, add 1/4 cup chicken broth and a tablespoon of butter to the pan to create a chile sauce. Serve with white rice.

1 1/2 pounds large shrimp, peeled and deveined
1/3 cup Red Chile Paste (page 100)
3 tablespoons olive oil
Salt and black pepper
2 limes, each cut into 4 wedges
Cilantro sprigs, for garnish

MARINATE THE SHRIMP

Start by soaking eight wooden skewers (see Cooking Notes). Thread the shrimp onto the skewers, leaving a small gap between each shrimp, which will allow them to cook evenly. You should be able to fit about four shrimp per skewer. Place the shrimp skewers in a large plastic freezer bag and spread the chile paste over the shrimp. Seal the bag, making sure to remove as much air as possible. Work the bag to evenly distribute the paste and rub it onto the shrimp. Place the bag in the refrigerator and allow the shrimp to marinate for 30 minutes.

GRILL OR SAUTÉ THE SHRIMP

Remove the shrimp skewers from the freezer bag. Drizzle both sides of the shrimp with 2 tablespoons oil and season with salt and pepper.

Preheat a grill to medium-high for 10 minutes or preheat a grill pan over medium-high heat. Oil the grill pan or grill grates with the remaining oil. Grill the shrimp for 5 minutes on each side. If sautéing, place a large sauté pan over medium-high heat and add the remaining oil. Add the shrimp skewers and cook for 5 minutes on each side. If the skewers do not fit in a single layer, sauté them in batches.

GARNISH AND SERVE

Spear a lime wedge onto the tip of each skewer. Place the shrimp skewers on a serving platter and top with sprigs of cilantro.

Seared Mahi Mahi Salpicón

Salpicón—a shredded mixture of fish with herbs and seasonings—is traditionally made with left-over fish that is tossed with fresh ingredients and used as a filling for tacos or a topping for tostadas. I find the sauce so delicious that I like to pair it with freshly seared fish and let it stand on its own. Definitely keep the sauce in mind for times when you do have leftovers! **SERVES 4**

2 large tomatoes, cored and chopped

$1/2$ cup lightly packed fresh cilantro leaves, chopped, plus additional sprigs for garnish

2 tablespoons capers

$1^1/2$ teaspoons juice from caper jar

1 tablespoon red wine vinegar

$1/4$ cup olive oil, plus more as needed

2 cloves garlic, crushed

2 bay leaves

1 onion, chopped

Salt and black pepper

1 pound mahi mahi (or any other white fish) fillets, skinless, cut into chunks

Cayenne pepper

COOKING NOTES
INGREDIENTS

Fish

Almost any white-fleshed fish goes well with this recipe. So feel free to use what you have on hand or what is fresh at the market.

Cut your fish into chunks or flake it while you cook it—either way, it is a stress-free recipe since you do not have to worry about your fish falling apart while trying to flip it. Of course, you can also serve the fish as steaks or fillets and spoon the sauce over it.

TECHNIQUES

Making a Warm Vinaigrette

Combining the hot oil and onion with the cool tomato and vinegar creates a warm vinaigrette. This chunky sauce can be used in a variety of different ways, such as a salad dressing or as an accompaniment to grilled chicken or beef.

ADVANCE PREPARATION

The sauce can be prepared a day in advance. While it is best to cook the fish soon before serving it, the sauce can be made and combined with leftover fish. Just shred or break apart the fish with a fork and combine it with the chunky sauce.

START PREPARING THE SAUCE

In a bowl, combine the tomatoes, chopped cilantro, capers, caper juice, and vinegar. Set aside.

SAUTÉ THE ONION AND GARLIC

Place a large sauté pan over medium heat and add the olive oil, garlic, and bay leaves. When the garlic begins to sizzle, remove it from the pan and discard. Add the onion, season with 1 teaspoon salt and black pepper to taste, and cook until the onion is limp and translucent, about 8 minutes. Remove the bay leaves and pour the onions (along with most of the oil) into the bowl holding the tomato mixture. Toss well. Taste for seasoning and adjust if needed.

PREPARE AND SEAR THE FISH

Season the fish with salt and cayenne pepper. Take the same pan that was used to sauté the onion and place it over medium-high heat. Make sure there is at least 1 tablespoon of oil in the pan; add more if necessary.

Sear the fish for 3 to 4 minutes per side or until the fish is cooked through. Most fish will begin to flake at this point. Don't worry if the fish begins to fall apart—that is part of the look of the dish.

GARNISH AND SERVE

Transfer the cooked fish to a serving platter. Pour the warm tomato salad over the fish and garnish with sprigs of cilantro.

Snapper a la Veracruzana

Although originally from the Mexican state of Veracruz, Snapper a la Veracruzana is served all over the country. Clearly Mexicans know a good thing when they see it! A light tomato broth poaches the fish, while jalapeño, capers, and olives deliver a flavorful punch. This is a great choice for a family meal or a dinner party because the sauce can be made ahead of time, leaving only the fish to simmer in it. Quick and delicious! **SERVES 4**

3 tablespoons olive oil

1 onion, sliced

3 cloves garlic, minced

4 large (about 2 pounds) tomatoes, cored and chopped

10 pimiento-stuffed green olives, quartered

1 tablespoon capers

2 pickled jalapeños, stemmed and sliced

1 tablespoon pickled jalapeño juice from jar

2 bay leaves

2 sprigs fresh marjoram, plus more for garnish

1 teaspoon dried oregano

$^1/_2$ cup dry white wine

1 teaspoon salt, plus more to taste

$1^1/_2$ pounds red snapper, cut into 4 pieces

Black pepper

COOKING NOTES

INGREDIENTS

Fish

While snapper is the traditional choice, any firm white fish, such as sea bass, cod, grouper, or halibut, would also work well.

TECHNIQUES

Oven or Stovetop Cooking

While this dish is traditionally cooked on the stovetop, it can also be baked in the oven after the sauce has been made. It is a good idea if you are short on stovetop space or if you want to prepare the dish ahead of time. Preheat the oven to 350°F, place the seasoned fish fillets in an ovenproof baking dish, and top with the sauce. Bake for 20 minutes and garnish as instructed.

ADVANCE PREPARATION

The sauce can be made up to 2 days in advance and kept in the refrigerator.

PREPARE THE SAUCE

Heat the oil in a large sauté pan over medium heat. When the oil is hot, add the onion and garlic and sauté for about 5 minutes, until the onion is limp and translucent.

Add the tomatoes, olives, capers, pickled jalapeños along with the juice, bay leaves, marjoram, oregano, wine, and salt and stir well. Cook, uncovered, over medium heat for 30 minutes. Taste for seasoning and adjust if needed.

ADD THE FISH TO THE SAUCE

Season the fish fillets with salt and pepper and slide them into the simmering sauce, making sure to submerge the fillets under the liquid as much as possible. Cook for 10 minutes. (If the fish was not fully submerged, carefully turn the fillets over after 5 minutes and continue to cook.)

GARNISH AND SERVE

To serve, spoon a good portion of the sauce onto a dish or platter and place the fillets over it. Top with a helping of the sauce and garnish with sprigs of fresh marjoram.

Fish Tacos

Tacos have been part of Mexico's culinary heritage for well over a hundred years. These folded tortillas can be stuffed with any number of fillings—with each Mexican state claiming stake to their own. Fish tacos are said to come from Baja California, Mexico's northernmost state. While the original fish taco was made with deep-fried fish, this recipe—made with sautéed fish—is a delicious and fresh version. This recipe is easily doubled, which makes it a great dish to make when entertaining a crowd. **SERVES 4**

1/2 red onion, thinly sliced

About 1 1/2 cups red wine vinegar

1/4 cup olive oil

1 1/2 teaspoons ancho chile powder

1 1/2 teaspoons dried oregano

1/2 teaspoon ground cumin

1/4 cup lightly packed fresh cilantro leaves, chopped, plus more for garnish

1 jalapeño, stemmed and chopped

1 pound flaky white fish (such as mahi mahi or cod), cut into 4 pieces

Salt

8 fresh corn tortillas

Mexican crema, homemade (page 102) or store-bought

Fresh Tomato Salsa (page 96)

2 limes, cut into quarters

COOKING NOTES

INGREDIENTS

Fish

You can use any fish you like so long as you can flake the flesh when it is cooked. Most white fish fall under this category.

TECHNIQUES

Marinated Onions

Once you make this very simple condiment, you will find yourself keeping a container of these onions in your refrigerator to add to all of your dishes.

Don't be alarmed by the amount of vinegar needed to cover the onions completely. Since you will most likely have onions leftover, keep them submerged in the vinegar in a refrigerated airtight container. You can then use the vinegar for your other cooking needs. The onions will keep for several weeks.

ADVANCE PREPARATION

The onions and fish can be made up to a day in advance. When reheating the fish, you may want to add about 1 tablespoon of water to make sure the fish does not dry out.

MARINATE THE ONION

Put the onion in a small bowl and pour in enough red wine vinegar to cover well. Set aside for at least 30 minutes or up to several weeks.

MARINATE THE FISH

Pour the olive oil into a small bowl and add the ancho chile powder, oregano, cumin, chopped cilantro, and jalapeño. Mix well. Place the fish on a dish and pour the marinade over it, making sure to coat the fish well on both sides. Allow to marinate for 20 minutes.

COOK THE FISH

Heat a nonstick sauté pan over medium-high heat. Remove the fish from the marinade and place in the hot pan (there is no need to add more oil). Season the fish with salt. Cook the fish for 4 minutes undisturbed, then turn over, and cook for another 2 minutes. Remove the pan from the heat and flake the fish into the pan with a fork, making sure to mix in all the marinade that has stuck to the bottom of the pan. Check for seasoning and add more salt if necessary. Set aside.

HEAT THE TORTILLAS

Place four of the tortillas on a plate and sandwich them between two slightly dampened sheets of paper towel. Microwave on high for 45 seconds. Place the warm tortillas in a towel-lined basket or plate and cover. Repeat with the remaining tortillas.

ASSEMBLE AND SERVE

To assemble the tacos, place a heaping spoonful of the marinated flaked fish onto the center of a tortilla. Top with the marinated onions. Serve accompanied by Mexican crema and salsa.

Garnish with lime wedges and cilantro sprigs.

Seared Tuna with Tomato and Roasted Corn Salsa

This recipe serves you summer on a dish. You will see how the tomato and roasted corn salsa pop right off the plate. While the salsa pairs beautifully with the tuna, feel free to pair it with your favorite fish or even chicken. Fast, fresh, and easy—this will soon become your quick dinner fix. **SERVES 4**

COOKING NOTES

INGREDIENTS

Frozen Corn

If you are using frozen corn, measure the amount needed before defrosting.

Tuna Steaks

Try to buy a very thick piece of tuna—ideally $1^1/_2$ inches thick. This will allow you to achieve a nice golden brown crust while maintaining a rare center.

TECHNIQUES

Searing Tuna

Searing fish on a hot griddle or skillet is the best way to achieve a golden crust while maintaining a moist interior. While grilling is very popular, I find that it dries out the fish too much. To properly sear, make sure you start off with a hot pan and oil. Place the meat in the pan and leave it alone until it develops a golden brown crust.

Roasting Corn

For this recipe, you are looking to do more than just cook the corn through. You want to caramelize its sugars—making it sweet—and change its texture—making it crunchy. Leave the corn in the oven until its color changes from yellow to a deep golden brown.

ADVANCE PREPARATION

The salsa can be made up to a day in advance, although it is best to keep the corn separate so as to maintain its crunchy texture.

The tuna can be made a couple of hours ahead of time, stored in the refrigerator, and served at room temperature.

Kernels cut from 2 ears corn, or 1 cup frozen corn kernels, defrosted (see Cooking Notes, page 14)

2 tablespoons olive oil

$1/_2$ teaspoon salt, plus more to taste

Black pepper

1 cup cherry tomatoes, quartered

2 scallions, white portion only, chopped

$1/_4$ cup lightly packed fresh cilantro leaves, chopped, plus more for garnish

1 avocado, pitted and chopped (see Cooking Notes, page 10)

2 limes

1 pound tuna steak

Cayenne pepper

ROAST THE CORN

Preheat the oven to 450°F. Prepare a baking sheet by lining it with parchment paper or aluminum foil.

Put the corn kernels on the baking sheet and toss with 1 tablespoon of the olive oil, $1/_4$ teaspoon of the salt, and black pepper to taste. Spread the corn out evenly on the baking sheet and roast for 20 minutes. You want the corn to take on a golden brown color. It may seem that you have left the corn in the oven for too long, but you want the corn to caramelize and get a little crunchy. Remove the corn from the oven and set aside.

PREPARE THE SALSA

While the corn is roasting, combine the tomatoes, scallions, cilantro, and avocado in a bowl. Finely grate the zest of 1 lime and add it, along with its juice, to the bowl. Toss well.

Once the corn is ready, toss it in the tomato mixture and season with $1/_4$ teaspoon of the salt. Taste and adjust the seasoning as needed. Set aside.

PREPARE THE TUNA

Using a paper towel, pat dry the tuna steak and season with a dusting of salt and cayenne.

continued on page 42

Heat the remaining 1 tablespoon oil in a nonstick grill pan over medium-high heat. When the oil is hot, add the tuna and cook to medium-rare, turning once. The time it will take for the tuna to cook depends on its thickness. If you're able to get a thick piece of tuna (about 1^1/$_2$ inches thick), allow the tuna to sear for 4 minutes on each side for a medium-rare doneness. Thinner steaks will cook in less time. Ultimately the tuna's thickness and your preferred level of doneness will determine how long to cook the fish.

ASSEMBLE THE DISH
Cut the remaining lime into wedges. Serve the tuna along with the tomato and roasted corn salsa and garnish each serving with a lime wedge and sprigs of cilantro.

Smothered Shrimp Tostadas

The shrimp in this recipe are cooked in a manner that is referred to as *enchilado*, or in a chile sauce. While the shrimp go well served atop crisp fresh lettuce and a crunchy tortilla, they can also be served over a bed of white rice with extra sauce drizzled on top. Either way, you will find the shrimp to be as versatile as they are delicious. **SERVES 4**

2 large (about 1 pound) tomatoes

2 cloves garlic, unpeeled

1 canned chipotle chile, seeds removed if desired

1 teaspoon red wine vinegar

$1/2$ teaspoon salt, plus more to taste

1 pound large shrimp, peeled, deveined, and butterflied

1 tablespoon olive oil

12 flat tostada shells, packaged or homemade (see Cooking Notes, page 8)

1 head lettuce (such as iceberg, romaine, bibb, or green leaf), finely shredded

1 cup Mexican crema, homemade (page 102) or store-bought

$1/4$ cup lightly packed fresh cilantro leaves, chopped

ROAST THE TOMATOES AND GARLIC

Place a nonstick or cast-iron skillet over medium-high heat and add the tomato and garlic. Roast for about 15 minutes, until the tomatoes are completely roasted and soft. Turn the tomato every 4 minutes or so, until all sides are roasted and charred (parts of the tomato skin will blacken, but do not worry; that is what you want). Remove from heat and set aside. The garlic will begin to roast more slowly, but rotate it every 5 minutes or so. When the garlic starts to release its aroma, and becomes soft to the touch, it is ready. Remove from the skillet, let cool, and then peel (you can just squeeze the garlic out of its skin).

PREPARE THE SAUCE

Combine the whole tomatoes and garlic in a blender with the chipotle chile, vinegar, and salt. Puree until smooth.

SAUTÉ THE SHRIMP

Season the shrimp with salt. Heat the oil in a sauté pan over medium-high heat. When the oil is hot, add the shrimp and sauté until they are all golden brown, about 2 minutes.

Pour the chipotle sauce over the shrimp and stir to combine well. Allow to simmer for 5 minutes to blend the flavors and thicken the sauce. Check the seasoning and adjust if necessary. Remove from the heat and set aside while you begin to assemble the tostadas.

ASSEMBLE THE TOSTADAS

Note that it is not important to measure the tostada ingredients precisely. Use as much or as little as you like. Place a tostada on a dish and top with about $1/4$ cup (a handful) of shredded lettuce. Add 3 or 4 shrimp to the tostada along with some extra chipotle sauce. Drizzle some crema over the shrimp and garnish with fresh cilantro. Repeat until all the tostadas are assembled.

COOKING NOTES
TECHNIQUES

Butterflying Shrimp

Tostadas tend to be eaten with the hands, so it is a good idea to make sure all ingredients are bite size. For this reason, it is best to butterfly the shrimp prior to cooking. This will not only make it easier to eat, but the shrimp will absorb the flavors of the sauce more intensely and cook more quickly.

A butterflied shrimp is a shrimp that has been sliced lengthwise. In some cases, one side of the shrimp is kept attached, but other times it is sliced all the way through. For this recipe, the shrimp will be sliced in half all the way through.

Peel and devein the shrimp. Place a shrimp on your cutting board and hold your knife blade along the indentation found along the back of the shrimp (the site of the deveining). Slice the shrimp in half lengthwise using the indentation as your guide.

ADVANCE PREPARATION

While it is best to assemble the tostadas just before serving, you can make the shrimp and the sauce in advance. The sauce can be made a day ahead and the shrimp can be cooked a few hours before you plan to serve them. If you are cooking the shrimp ahead of time, try to undercook them a bit so that when they are reheated they don't become tough.

Chicken

Achiote Chicken Roasted in Banana Leaves

I hope the banana leaves will entice—not discourage—you from making this recipe. The leaves may be tricky to find, but they are worth it. Available in most Latin markets or through online sources, the banana leaves give off an intoxicating smokiness you cannot get from any other ingredient. This simple recipe can also be made with fish and shellfish. For this recipe, you will need five 12-inch squares of banana leaves. **SERVES 4**

COOKING NOTES
INGREDIENTS

Banana Leaves

These are most commonly found frozen. To use, just thaw at room temperature and unfold. Whether you are using fresh or frozen, you want to make sure you cut off the spine that runs through the leaf because it will prevent you from folding it properly.

If you are using the frozen leaves, you will notice that each package holds a good number of leaves. After defrosting the package and using the leaves that are needed, repack the leaves in plastic wrap, making sure to create an airtight package, and return to the freezer. You can defrost and refreeze the leaves as often as you need. It will not affect the flavor or texture of these hearty leaves.

TECHNIQUES

Using a Substitute for Banana Leaves

You can substitute 12-inch squares of aluminum foil or parchment paper for banana leaves. The ultimate flavor of the dish will be altered slightly, but it will still be delicious.

Grilling Packets

The packets can also be cooked in an outdoor grill. Heat your grill to medium-high and place the packets on it, seam side down. Close the grill cover and allow to cook for 30 minutes.

ADVANCE PREPARATION

The packages can be made early in the day and left in the refrigerator until you are ready for them.

SERVING SUGGESTIONS

This dish can be served on individual plates or on a platter on a buffet table. In both cases, allow your guest to open the banana-leaf packages themselves. They will not only be impressed with the presentation, they will be intoxicated by the smoky aroma.

4 skinless chicken breasts (about 1 1/4 pounds)
1/2 cup Achiote Marinade (page 92)
Salt and black pepper

MARINATE THE CHICKEN

Put the chicken in a sealable plastic bag and pour in the marinade. Seal the bag and distribute the marinade evenly over the chicken. Place in the refrigerator for 30 minutes.

FORM PACKETS USING THE BANANA LEAVES

Remove the marinated chicken from the refrigerator. Lay a banana leaf in front of you, making sure the shiny side is facing up. Place a chicken breast with marinade still clinging to it in the center of the leaf and season with salt and pepper. Fold one side of the leaf over the chicken. Overlap the opposite side over the leaf. Fold the two ends in toward the center and place the package—seam side down—on a baking sheet. Tear a long thin strip from an extra piece of banana leaf and tie it around the chicken-stuffed package to secure it. Repeat with the remaining chicken.

ROAST THE PACKETS

Preheat the oven to 350°F.

Prepare a baking sheet by lining it with aluminum foil. Place the chicken packets on the baking sheet in a single layer.

Roast the chicken packets for 30 minutes. Remove from oven and allow to sit for 5 minutes before opening.

SERVE

The chicken should be served in its banana leaf wrapper and opened by guests at the table.

1. Remove the spine from the banana leaf, then place it in front of you, shiny side up.

2. Place the filling in the center of the leaf and fold one side over it.

3. Fold over the other side of the leaf.

4. Secure the top of the folded package with your fingers and place your thumbs under the bottom of the package.

5. Use your thumbs to fold up the bottom of the package.

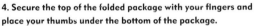

6. Continue turning the package over so that the seam is facing down.

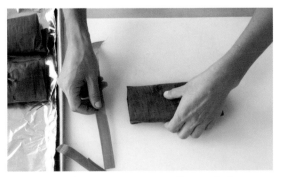

7. Tear a long strip from an extra piece of banana leaf.

8. Tie the strip around the package in a knot to secure it.

Chicken Tamales with Tomatillo-Cilantro Sauce

While tamales are one of Mexico's most famous street foods, they are also one of its most popular party foods, which is fitting since a tamal is packaged like a small gift waiting to be unwrapped. The many steps involved in tamal making have discouraged countless cooks. But they should not, because the process is very easy. And if you gather a few friends to help with the assembling, you can have a tamal-making party before the real party begins. **MAKES 24 TAMALES**

CHICKEN
1 onion, halved
2 cloves garlic, crushed
1/2 teaspoon salt
5 cups water
1 pound (about 3 breasts) boneless, skinless
    chicken breasts
2 bay leaves
1 teaspoon dried oregano

POACH AND SHRED THE CHICKEN
Combine the onion, garlic, salt, and water in a saucepan and bring to a boil. Add the chicken breasts, bay leaves, and oregano and decrease the heat to a simmer. Cook the chicken, partially covered, for 35 minutes, or until cooked through. To check for doneness, slit the chicken in half to make sure the interior is no longer pink.

COOKING NOTES
INGREDIENTS

Lard versus Shortening

For a truly authentic taste, you must use freshly rendered lard. If you buy commercial lard, make sure it is fresh, refrigerated lard; otherwise use vegetable shortening, which still produces a very good tamal.

TECHNIQUES

Poaching Chicken

You will end up with a juicier chicken if you allow it to cool in the broth. Make sure you save the broth, because it has a wonderful flavor that you will want to use when making the tamal dough.

Working with Corn Husks

Be careful not to open corn husks when they are dry because they will split and break. After soaking them in hot water, wrap in a damp paper towel until you are ready to use them. If they cool down and dry out before you are ready to use them, submerge them in hot water for a few minutes until pliable.

Allow the chicken to cool in the broth. When cool enough to handle, remove the chicken from the pan. Strain and reserve the broth. Shred the chicken by hand by pulling apart the fibers of the chicken with your fingers and set aside.

TOMATILLO-CILANTRO SAUCE
8 tomatillos, husks removed, rinsed, and quartered
    (see Cooking Notes, page 73)
2 to 3 jalapeños, stemmed and halved
1 cup lightly packed fresh cilantro, tender stems
    and leaves
1 clove garlic
2 tablespoons water
1 tablespoon olive oil
1 onion, sliced
Salt and black pepper

About 30 corn husks

MAKE THE TOMATILLO-CILANTRO SAUCE
Combine the tomatillos, jalapeños, cilantro, garlic, and water in a blender and puree until well blended.

Heat the oil in a sauté pan over medium heat. When the oil is hot, add the onion and sauté until the onion is limp and translucent, about 8 minutes. Add the tomatillo mixture. Season with salt and pepper. Cook for about 5 minutes, or until the sauce thickens.

Add the shredded chicken to the sauce and stir to coat. Allow to cook for 3 more minutes. Check the seasoning and adjust if needed. Set aside.

PREPARE THE CORN HUSKS
Bring a large pot of water to a boil then remove from heat. Add the corn husks, making sure to submerge them under water, and cover the pot. Soak the corn husks in the pot for 20 minutes. They should be soft and flexible, and take on a deep beige color. Remove the corn husks from the water and wrap them in a damp paper towel until you are ready to use them.

continued on page 50

TAMAL DOUGH

2½ cups masa harina (cornmeal for tamales; Maseca brand is recommended)

2 cups plus 3 tablespoons chicken broth (reserved from poaching chicken)

¾ cup fresh lard or solid vegetable shortening

1 teaspoon baking powder

2 teaspoons salt

GARNISH

Mexican crema, homemade (page 102) or store-bought

PREPARE THE TAMAL DOUGH

To make the masa, combine the masa harina with 2 cups of the reserved chicken broth and mix well. The masa should have the consistency of a stiff dough. Set aside.

Put the lard in a mixing bowl. Beat the lard with an electric mixer until light and fluffy, about 1 minute. Add half of the masa and beat until well blended. Add the 3 tablespoons of the reserved chicken broth and the remaining masa and continue beating until a teaspoon of the dough dropped into a cup of cold water floats, about 10 minutes. If after 15 minutes of

---

COOKING NOTES
ADVANCE PREPARATION

Reheating Tamales

Cooked tamales can be refrigerated for a couple of days and reheated in a steamer or in the microwave. If you are using the microwave, put the tamales in a bowl and pour in ¼ inch of water. Seal with plastic wrap and heat for 2 minutes. The steam created within the plastic will reheat the tamales. If reheating in a steamer, recreate the tamal steamer explained in the recipe and steam for 5 minutes.

Assembled but uncooked tamales can be frozen. When you are ready to serve them, steam them straight from the freezer for 1 hour 20 minutes (twice the cooking time). Do not defrost before cooking.

VARIATIONS

You can fill tamales with any number of different ingredients. In this book, you can use the recipe for Mexican chorizo (page 71), Seared Mahi Mahi Salpicón (page 36), and Roasted Chiles, Onions & Tomatoes (page 88).

---

constant beating your dough does not float, move on (despite it not floating, the dough will be fine).

Sprinkle the baking powder and the salt over the dough and mix in well.

ASSEMBLE THE TAMALES

Place a corn husk lengthwise in front of you with the wide side closest to you. Spread 2 tablespoons of the dough all over the bottom half (wide side) of the corn husk, leaving about a 1-inch-wide border on the left and right sides.

Place 2 heaping tablespoons of the filling lengthwise down the center of the dough. Pick up the two long sides of the cornhusk and unite them. Allow the dough to surround the filling by pinching together the corn husk where the dough comes together. Roll both sides of the corn husks in the same direction over the tamal. Fold down the empty top section of the cornhusk and secure it by tying a thin strip of corn husk around the tamal (the top will be open).

Repeat this process until all the corn husks or tamal dough are used up.

STEAM THE TAMALES

Create a tamal steamer by crumpling a large piece of aluminum foil into a large ball. Place the foil ball in the center of a large saucepan and arrange the tamales "standing up" around it. You can stand tamales in front of each other; just make sure that the open end of the tamal is facing upward.

Pour in ½ inch of water. Cover tightly with a lid and simmer for 40 minutes.

SERVE

Serve warm accompanied by Mexican crema.

1. Assemble all of your ingredients.

2. Rehydrate the cornhusks and prepare the tamal dough and chicken filling.

3. Spread the tamal dough all over the bottom half (the wide side) of a rehydrated cornhusk, leaving a 1-inch-wide border on the left and right side.

4. Place a mound of the filling lengthwise down the center of the dough.

5. Pick up the sides of the cornhusk and unite them, allowing the dough to surround the filling. Pinch the dough together.

6. Fold the flaps of the cornhusks over to one side.

7. Fold over the empty top section of the cornhusk.

8. Secure by tying a thin strip of cornhusk around the tamal.

9. Create a tamal steamer by placing a large piece of crumbled foil in the center of a saucepan and standing the tamales around it.

Citrus-Marinated Chicken

This dish, also referred to as *escabeche*, owes it origin to the Spanish, who created the technique of frying or poaching fish or chicken and then marinating it in a citrus or vinegar mixture as a way of preserving the meat. Because the marinating process can take up to a day, it is left in the refrigerator and as a result is typically served cold or at room temperature. It makes a great dish for a picnic or an outdoor meal because it can be made well in advance and only gets better with time. **SERVES 6**

2$^1/_2$ pounds chicken, white and dark meat,
    skinless, bone-in or boneless
1 yellow cooking onion, halved
2 cloves garlic, crushed
1 teaspoon salt
2 tablespoons dried oregano
1 cup freshly squeezed orange juice
$^1/_2$ cup freshly squeezed lime juice (about 5 limes),
    plus extra limes for garnish
1 large red onion, thinly sliced
2 jalapeños, stemmed and sliced into rings
1 tablespoon ground cumin
$^1/_4$ cup olive oil

COOKING NOTES

INGREDIENTS

Chicken

Feel free to use all white or all dark meat in this recipe. It is also up to you if you want to use chicken that is still on the bone.

ADVANCE PREPARATION

This dish is best when made in advance. The chicken can be left to marinate for 24 hours in the refrigerator.

NOTE

Using the Marinade as a Sauce

Because the chicken was cooked before it was placed in the marinade, it is safe to serve it as a sauce.

POACH THE CHICKEN

Put the chicken, yellow onion, garlic, salt, and 1 tablespoon of the oregano in a large saucepan and add enough water to barely cover the chicken. Bring the mixture to a boil, reduce to a simmer, and continue cooking, uncovered, for 30 minutes, or until cooked through. To check for doneness, slit the chicken in half to make sure the interior is no longer pink. Allow the chicken to cool in the broth.

Remove the chicken from the broth and cut it up into 2-inch chunks, if using boneless chicken. If you are using chicken on the bone, remove the white meat from the bone but leave the dark meat as is. Put the chicken pieces in a large bowl or deep dish.

Strain the broth and keep it for another use.

MARINATE THE CHICKEN

Combine the orange juice, lime juice, red onion, jalapeños, cumin, and the remaining 1 tablespoon oregano in a saucepan. Stir until well combined. Bring to a boil over high heat. Immediately remove it from the heat and add the olive oil. Pour the marinade into the bowl with the chicken and allow the chicken to marinate for at least 30 minutes, and up to 1 day, covered with plastic wrap and refrigerated. Try to turn the chicken pieces a few times during the marinating process.

GARNISH AND SERVE

Transfer the chicken to a deep platter and pour the marinade over it. Garnish with lime wedges.

Red Mole Chicken with Chorizo

Mexicans refer to this dish as *manchamanteles* or "tablecloth stainer" due to the delicious deep red sauce that is made from dried chiles and spices. The sauce has an underlying sweetness that is very addicting. And because this dish improves with age, you can make it days in advance or enjoy leftovers days later. **SERVES 4 TO 6**

4 dried ancho chiles

2 tablespoons olive oil, plus more as needed

4 cloves garlic, crushed

1 onion, chopped

1 pound fresh Mexican chorizo (page 71), or store-bought, casing removed

1 pound (about 3) boneless, skinless chicken breasts, cubed

Salt and black pepper

Pinch of ground cloves

$1/2$ teaspoon ground cinnamon

2 tablespoons cider vinegar

2 green (unripe) bananas, peeled and sliced

1 tablespoon sugar

1 teaspoon salt

$1/8$ teaspoon black pepper

Hot cooked white rice

ROAST AND SOAK THE CHILES

Tear the chiles into flat pieces and remove the veins and seeds. Put in a skillet over medium heat and roast the chiles on both sides until they begin to release their aroma and soften a bit, about 1 minute.

Transfer the chiles to a blender jar. Fill with boiling water. Soak for 30 minutes. Drain the water from the jar, reserving $1^{1}/_{2}$ cups water for use in the sauce. Leave the chiles in the blender.

BROWN THE VEGETABLES AND MEAT

Pour the olive oil into a large saucepan, add the garlic, and gradually warm the oil over medium heat. Add the onion and sauté for about 6 minutes, or until the onion is soft and translucent. Add to the blender.

Add the chorizo to the saucepan and cook for 1 minute over medium-high heat, or until it releases its fat. Dry the chicken breasts with a paper towel and season with salt and pepper. Add to the saucepan and brown for 4 minutes per side. Remove the chicken and chorizo from the saucepan and set aside.

MAKE THE SAUCE

Add the cloves, cinnamon, and 1 cup of the reserved water to the blender with the chiles, onion, and garlic. Blend to a smooth puree.

Make sure the bottom of the saucepan is coated with fat. If not, add a couple tablespoons of olive oil and place over medium-high heat. When the saucepan is hot, add the puree all at once and let it "fry" for 5 minutes, stirring constantly, until it becomes dark and thick.

ADD THE MEAT AND FINISH THE DISH

Add the chicken and chorizo to the saucepan along with the vinegar and the remaining reserved water. Season with the salt and pepper. Stir well and allow to simmer for 10 minutes, partially covered. Add the banana and the sugar and simmer for 5 minutes. Taste for seasoning; it should be slightly sweet.

SERVE

Serve warm over a bed of white rice.

Chicken Enchiladas with Tomatillo Sauce

I promise these enchiladas are unlike any you have ever had before. Although the tortillas are fried, the enchiladas are light and vibrantly flavorful because they are not smothered in cream and cheese. Instead the fresh cheese is crumbled on top and the tangy Mexican crema is served on the side.

SERVES 4 TO 6

1 pound (about 3) boneless, skinless chicken breasts
2 cloves garlic, slightly crushed
2 onions, halved
2 bay leaves
1 teaspoon dried oregano
$^1/_2$ teaspoon salt, plus more to taste
2 cups Fresh Tomatillo Sauce (page 95)

$^1/_3$ cup plus 1 tablespoon olive oil
Black pepper
12 fresh corn tortillas
Cilantro sprigs for garnish
$^1/_3$ cup crumbled queso fresco or feta cheese
1 cup Mexican crema, homemade (page 102) or store-bought
$^1/_2$ head iceberg lettuce, shredded

COOKING NOTES
TECHNIQUES

Frying the Tortillas

This recipe calls for frying the tortillas. This not only adds to their flavor and texture, but it also allows you to roll them up without tearing them.

In order to get crispy tortillas, the oil they are fried in must be very hot. Test the oil by dipping a piece of a tortilla in it. If it sizzles, it is ready. If it just bubbles, it is not ready. Keep heating the oil until it sizzles.

If you do not want to fry the tortillas, you can steam them instead. Place about four tortillas at a time in between two moist paper towels and heat in a microwave for about 30 seconds. Dip the steamed tortillas in the warm tomatillo sauce and continue with the recipe as instructed.

VARIATION

Chicken Enchiladas with Fresh Tomato Sauce

Simply substituting the fresh tomatillo sauce with the Fresh Tomato Sauce (page 98) will create the popular "red enchiladas."

ADVANCE PREPARATION

The enchiladas can be assembled about an hour ahead of time and placed in an ovenproof dish. Pour any remaining tomatillo sauce over the enchiladas and cover the dish with aluminum foil. Place in a warm (200°F) oven until you are ready to serve. Garnish as instructed.

POACH THE CHICKEN

Combine the chicken breasts, garlic, 1 onion, bay leaves, oregano, and $^1/_2$ teaspoon of salt in a saucepan. Add enough water to cover the chicken and bring to a boil. Decrease the heat to a simmer and cook for 35 minutes. To check for doneness, slit the chicken in half to make sure the interior is no longer pink; the juices should run clear.

Allow the chicken to cool in the broth (this will keep it moist). When it is cool enough to handle, shred the chicken by hand by pulling apart the fibers of the chicken with your fingers.

SAUTÉ THE ONION

Slice the remaining onion. Heat 1 tablespoon of the oil in a sauté pan over medium-high heat. When the oil is hot, add the onion and sauté until it becomes limp and translucent.

Toss the chicken with the onion and season with salt and pepper. Transfer to a bowl and set aside.

PREPARE THE TORTILLAS AND ASSEMBLE THE ENCHILADAS

To build the enchiladas, you will need to create a three-part assembly line made up of two sauté pans and the bowl containing the shredded chicken and onion. You will also need to have an empty plate and the serving platter on hand.

First, heat the remaining $^1/_3$ cup oil in a sauté pan over medium-high heat. Next, pour the tomatillo sauce into the other sauté pan and place over medium heat.

continued on page 56

Now the assembly line: Working with one tortilla at a time, dip a tortilla in the oil and allow it to fry for 15 seconds on each side. Transfer the lightly fried tortilla to the saucepan holding the tomatillo sauce and coat well with the sauce. Transfer to the empty plate, place about ¹/₄ cup of the shredded chicken in the center, and roll. Place the enchilada on a serving platter seam side down. Repeat with the remaining tortillas.

Once you have finished assembling the enchiladas, pour any remaining tomatillo sauce over the enchiladas and top with sprigs of cilantro and crumbled queso fresco. Serve with Mexican crema and shredded lettuce alongside.

Stacked Chicken Tostadas

One of the best characteristics of the Mexican kitchen is that many recipes are an assembly of ingredients and often use up leftovers. This is one such recipe. If you think of a tostada as an edible plate, you will realize the endless options for creating them. A meal is usually made up of two tostadas, which I like to stack because placing them side-by-side looks a bit awkward on a plate. And remember, tostadas are usually eaten with your hands! **SERVES 6**

COOKING NOTES
INGREDIENTS

Tostadas

You can buy commercial tostada shells or fry your own. Commercial tostada shells are basically large tortilla chips. Buy your favorite brand, but try to find tostadas that are 6 to 9 inches wide, round, and flat.

Tostada Toppings

The toppings listed in this recipe are only a guide. Feel free to eliminate or substitute any ingredient. And use as much or as little of them as you please.

TECHNIQUES

Homemade Tostadas

To make homemade fried tortillas for tostadas, purchase 6-inch corn tortillas. Pour 2 inches of olive oil into a shallow pan and heat over medium high heat. When the oil is hot, add the tortillas, one at a time, and fry until golden brown on both sides. Remove from the pan, place in a paper towel–lined dish, and sprinkle with salt.

POACHED CHICKEN

1 onion, halved

2 cloves garlic, crushed

¹/₂ teaspoon salt, plus more to taste

5 cups water

1¹/₂ pounds (about 5) boneless, skinless chicken breasts

2 bay leaves

2 teaspoons dried oregano

COOKING NOTES
ADVANCE PREPARATION

All of the toppings can be prepared well in advance and the tostada assembled just before serving.

An option when serving tostadas is to set out all the toppings and allow your guests to create their own tostadas. That will not only ensure they get a tostada of their liking, but also that you will have made a stress-free meal.

TOSTADA AND TOPPINGS

$1/2$ red onion, thinly sliced

About 1 cup red wine vinegar

12 flat tostada shells, packaged or homemade

1 avocado, pitted and chopped (see Cooking Notes, page 10)

1 plum tomato, chopped

$1/4$ cup lightly packed cilantro leaves, chopped, plus 6 sprigs for garnish

4 limes, 1 juiced and 3 quartered

Salt

1 head bibb or romaine lettuce, shredded

$1 1/2$ cups black beans (page 78), or canned, drained

1 cup crumbled queso fresco or feta cheese

$1/2$ cup Mexican crema, homemade (page 102) or store-bought

POACH AND SHRED THE CHICKEN

Combine the onion, garlic, $1/2$ teaspoon salt, and water in a saucepan and bring to a boil. Add the chicken breasts, bay leaves, and oregano and decrease the heat to a simmer. Cook the chicken, partially covered, for 35 minutes, until cooked through. To check for doneness, slit the chicken in half to make sure the interior is no longer pink; the juices should run clear.

Allow the chicken to cool in the broth. When cool enough to handle, remove the chicken from the pan. Shred the chicken by hand by pulling apart the fibers of the chicken with your fingers, and set aside. If desired, strain the broth and reserve for future use.

MARINATE THE ONION

Put the red onion in a small bowl and pour in enough red wine vinegar to cover well. Set aside for at least 30 minutes.

PREPARE THE SALAD

In a small bowl, toss together the avocado, tomato, cilantro, and juice of 1 lime. Season with salt to taste. Set aside.

ASSEMBLE THE TOSTADAS

The amount of ingredients used for the topping is up to you. You are going to create two tostadas and place one on top of the other, so do not overfill them or they will not stack up.

Place a tostada shell on a plate and top with shredded lettuce, marinated onion, shredded chicken, black beans, crumbles of queso fresco, and avocado-tomato salad. Drizzle some crema over it and top with a second tostada and toppings.

Once stacked, garnish the tostada sitting on top with a sprig of cilantro and serve with a lime wedge.

Meat

Achiote Pork Skewers

This recipe was inspired by the traditional *pibil*-style barbecued pork, in which entire pigs are marinated in an achiote marinade and cooked in an underground pit lined with banana leaves. While you won't need a pit or an entire pig, these pork skewers evoke the same smoky citrus flavor with much less time and effort. Note: You will need eight 6-inch wooden skewers for this recipe. **SERVES 4**

1 1/4 pounds pork loin or pork shoulder
1/2 cup Achiote Marinade (page 92)
1 onion, sliced
1 teaspoon salt
1/4 teaspoon black pepper
2 limes, cut into wedges

COOKING NOTES
INGREDIENTS

Pork

This method and marinade works well with various cuts of pork. I have tried it with both pork loin and pork shoulder with equal success. While the shoulder is incredibly flavorful and tender, it is fattier. If you want a leaner cut, you can go with the loin, which will not be as tender but will be equally flavorful.

TECHNIQUES

Reverse Braising

This technique, simmering meat in a liquid until it completely evaporates, then allowing the meat to brown in its juices, is used often in Mexican cooking. I have not been able to find a proper name for this cooking method, so I gave it one: reverse braise. Braising involves browning, then simmering; here it's the reverse.

Infusing with Banana Leaves

If you have a banana leaf, take one and place it over the simmering skewers. The smoky flavor of the leaf will infuse into the pork, giving it a classic Mexican barbecue touch.

ADVANCE PREPARATION

The pork skewers can be assembled up to one day in advance and left to marinate. The cooked skewers can be held, covered, in a warm (250°F) oven for about 1 hour.

PREPARE THE PORK

Cut the pork into 1-inch cubes and thread about 3 pieces onto each skewer. Place the pork skewers in a large resealable plastic bag and pour in the marinade, making sure to evenly distribute the marinade over the pork. Seal the plastic bag and place the pork in the refrigerator for at least 30 minutes, or up to 24 hours.

REVERSE BRAISE THE PORK

This is a great, no-stress technique. Remove the pork skewers from the plastic bag and place them in a shallow saucepan large enough to hold the pork in one layer. Pour the marinade remaining in the bag over the pork and sprinkle the sliced onions, salt, and pepper over the skewers. Add enough water to the pan to barely cover the pork.

Bring the water to a boil, then decrease the heat to a simmer. Continue cooking, uncovered, until approximately half of the liquid has evaporated, about 35 minutes. Turn the skewers over and continue simmering, uncovered, until all of the water has evaporated, about 20 minutes. At this point, you want to make sure the onions are spread out and some are touching the bottom of the pan.

Once all of the liquid has evaporated, continue cooking for another 8 to 10 minutes, turning the skewers on all four sides to make sure the meat is nicely browned.

SERVE

Place the skewers on a platter and serve with lime wedges.

Carne Asada Tacos

If you have ever eaten from a taco truck, you will know why carne asada (grilled beef) tacos are the ultimate Mexican street food. Charred crispy beef is wrapped in a warm and chewy corn tortilla and drizzled with your choice of fresh tomato or tomatillo sauce. It is easy to make and even easier to serve because you can have your guests make their own. **SERVES 4**

About 2 cups red wine vinegar

1 red onion, thinly sliced

1 pound skirt steak

1 clove garlic, halved

Salt and black pepper

2 limes

2 tablespoons olive oil

12 (6-inch) fresh corn tortillas

1 avocado, pitted and sliced (see Cooking Notes, page 73)

1 cup Fresh Tomato Salsa (page 96) or Fresh Tomatillo Sauce (page 95)

Cilantro sprigs, for garnish

COOKING NOTES

INGREDIENTS

Skirt Steak

The traditional cut for carne asada tacos is skirt steak because it is fatty enough to resist drying out over high heat, which allows you to get a nice char on your steak.

TECHNIQUES

Pounding the Steak

Pounding the meat not only tenderizes it, but it increases the meat surface area and allows you to season more of it, making for a more flavorful steak.

To easily pound the skirt steak, pound at a 45° angle (in other words, don't pound straight down) with a meat mallet and go with the grain (follow the muscle fibers).

ADVANCE PREPARATION

The sauces and marinated onions can be made up to a day in advance.

MARINATE THE ONION

Put the red onion in a small bowl and pour in enough red wine vinegar to cover well. Set aside for at least 30 minutes.

POUND AND MARINATE THE BEEF

Cut the skirt steak into 4 equal pieces. Using a meat mallet, pound the beef to a $1/4$-inch thickness.

If using an outdoor grill, preheat it now. Rub the cut side of the garlic clove all over the meat and season generously with salt and pepper. About 5 minutes before grilling, squeeze the juice of 1 lime over both sides of the beef.

GRILL THE BEEF

Place a grill pan over high heat and add the olive oil. (If using an outdoor grill, brush the grill with olive oil and set the heat to high.) Grill the beef for 4 minutes per side. Remove from the heat and let it rest for 5 minutes before chopping it into $1/2$-inch pieces.

HEAT THE TORTILLAS

Place four of the tortillas on a plate and sandwich them between two slightly dampened sheets of paper towel. Microwave on high for 45 seconds. Place the warm tortillas in a towel-lined basket or plate and cover. Repeat with the remaining tortillas.

ASSEMBLE AND SERVE

To assemble the tacos, place a heaping spoonful of the grilled skirt steak onto the center of a tortilla. Top with marinated onions and a slice of avocado. Serve accompanied by tomato salsa or tomatillo sauce.

Cut the remaining lime into wedges. Garnish with the lime wedges and cilantro sprigs.

Chile-Glazed Pork Chops with Fresh Tomatillo Sauce

These succulent pork chops are perfect for a small dinner party or family dinner at home. If you have the Red Chile Paste and Fresh Tomatillo Sauce made ahead of time, you will have dinner on the table before you know it. I like to serve these with the Shredded Cabbage & Radish Slaw (page 24). Comforting and flavorful—this is sure to become a family favorite. **SERVES 4**

COOKING NOTES
INGREDIENTS

Pork Chops

Because bone-in pork chops are more flavorful than boneless chops, I prefer them in this recipe. But feel free to use either one. I also like to use the thick cuts, but the thin ones also work well. Just make sure to decrease the braising time if you are using thin cuts because they will cook in less time.

TECHNIQUES

Braising the Pork Chop

Braising is a technique used to tenderize tough cuts of meat. The meat is first seared to develop a nice golden crust, then simmered in a liquid to cook it through without drying it out. You will find variations of this technique throughout the meat recipes in this book, as Mexican cooking tends to use tougher (and tastier) cuts of meat.

ADVANCE PREPARATION

The red chile paste and tomatillo sauce can be made well in advance (up to 3 days before). Once the pork chops are braised, they can be held, covered, in a warm (250°F) oven for about 1 hour before serving.

4 bone-in pork chops, ideally 1 inch thick and
    $^1/_2$ pound each
1 cup Red Chile Paste (page 100)
Salt and black pepper
2 tablespoons olive oil
About 3 cups beer or water
1 cup Fresh Tomatillo Sauce (page 95)

MARINATE THE PORK CHOPS

Slather both sides of the pork chops with the chile paste and place in a large resealable plastic bag. Allow to marinate in the refrigerator for at least 10 minutes (and up to a few hours).

SEAR THE PORK CHOPS

Leave a light coating of the chile paste on the pork chops and season with salt and pepper. Place a large, well-seasoned cast-iron or nonstick skillet over medium-high heat, and add the olive oil. When the oil is hot, add the pork chops in a single layer and sear for 2 minutes on each side, or until the meat turns golden brown.

BRAISE IN BEER

Pour in enough beer to barely cover the chops. Cover the pan (top with a piece of aluminum foil large enough to cover the pan if yours does not have a lid) and decrease the heat to a simmer. Cook for 15 minutes. Turn the pork chops over and cook for another 15 minutes.

REDUCE THE LIQUID TO A GLAZE

Uncover the skillet and increase the heat to medium-high. Allow the liquid to reduce almost completely, flipping the pork chops over every few minutes to ensure that both sides become glazed with the reduced sauce. This should take about 10 minutes.

SERVE

Serve warm with tomatillo sauce.

Chile-Smothered Spareribs

The most difficult part of making these ribs is waiting for them to be ready. And the best part is that they practically make themselves. It is said that ribs should be cooked low and slow, and this recipe does just that. Cumin, oregano, and chipotle chiles slowly infuse into the meat of these ribs for 3 hours before they are glazed with honey and adobo. A winning combination! **SERVES 4**

2 racks (about 5 pounds total) baby back ribs
    or spareribs
1/2 cup olive oil
4 canned chipotle chiles
2 teaspoons ground cumin
2 tablespoons dried oregano
4 cloves garlic
2 teaspoons salt, plus more to taste
1 teaspoon black pepper, plus more to taste
1 cup honey
1/2 cup adobo sauce from canned chipotles

PREPARE THE RIBS
Preheat the oven to 275°F. Position one oven rack on the bottom and the second one in the center of the oven.

Before getting started, make sure the bottom (the bony side) of the ribs are lightly scored (have small gashes). If they are not, create shallow 1-inch-long gashes throughout the bottom side of the rib racks. (This is to help the ribs cook evenly.)

MARINATE THE RIBS
Combine the olive oil, chipotle chiles, cumin, oregano, garlic, 2 teaspoons salt, and 1 teaspoon black pepper in a food processor or blender and process until you have a coarse puree. You may need to scrape down the side of the blender jar or processor bowl a few times.

Place a piece of plastic wrap that is a bit longer than the length of the ribs on your counter and put one of the rib racks in its center. Pour half of the marinade over the ribs and coat both sides well. Wrap the plastic securely around the rib rack.

Next, wrap a large piece of aluminum foil around the plastic-lined rib rack, making sure to cover all the plastic and seal it well. Repeat the same procedure with the second rack.

Allow to marinate in the refrigerator for at least 1 hour, or up to 24 hours.

ROAST

Fill a large roasting pan with 2 inches of water and place the pan on the bottom rack of the oven. Place the two foil-wrapped rib packages on an oven rack situated right above the pan filled with water and roast for 3 hours. Make sure to check on the water level every hour or so and refill as needed.

GLAZE

Remove both rib packages and the water-filled roasting pan from the oven and increase the oven temperature to 450°F.

In a small mixing bowl, combine the honey with the adobo sauce until well blended. Set aside.

Carefully remove the foil and plastic wrap from the rib racks and place the racks on a baking sheet lined with foil. Making sure the bony sides of the racks are facing up, brush half of the honey glaze over them. Roast for 10 minutes.

Turn the racks over, brush with half the remaining glaze, and roast for another 5 minutes.

Brush the rest of the glaze over the rib rack and return to the oven for a final 5 minutes or until the ribs are a dark golden brown.

Remove the ribs from the oven and allow them to rest for 10 minutes before slicing into individual ribs.

SERVE

Transfer the ribs to a serving platter and serve.

COOKING NOTES

INGREDIENTS

Baby Back Ribs versus Spareribs

Ribs can come from either the underbelly or the back (loin section) of the pig. Spareribs come from the underbelly, and have less meat, more fat, and more flavor than baby back ribs, which come from the loin section. St. Louis–style ribs are trimmed spareribs. Feel free to use whichever cut you prefer.

TECHNIQUES

Roasting the Ribs in Steam

Roasting the ribs in a steam oven serves two purposes. First, it helps infuse the ribs with the flavors of the marinade. Second, it helps tenderize them.

Wrapping the racks first in plastic and then in aluminum foil also helps to maximize the flavor and texture of the ribs by keeping the marinade in close contact with the meat and not allowing it to dry out during the 3-hour roast. The foil layer is there to keep the plastic wrap from melting. Because the oven is set at a low temperature and there is steam being produced in it, there is no danger of the plastic wrap melting. However, do not attempt this technique with a higher oven temperature.

Glazing

You can glaze the ribs in the oven as the recipe states or on an outdoor grill.

ADVANCE PREPARATION

The longer you marinate the ribs, the more flavorful they will be. Ideally you should marinate them for 24 hours.

You can roast the ribs a few hours before you plan to serve them and keep them wrapped in the foil until you are ready to glaze.

Meatballs in Chipotle Sauce

Meatballs are the ultimate comfort food. And while these are satisfyingly delicious, they also pack a spicy punch. The chipotles add an unexpected smoky heat to the tomato sauce, which only gets better with time. So make them in advance for a no-stress meal, and make sure to make extra so you can have some for leftovers. **SERVES 6**

COOKING NOTES
INGREDIENTS

Canned Chipotles

You can adjust the spiciness of this sauce by adding more or fewer chipotle chiles and removing their seeds (the seeds are what contribute the heat).

Ground Meat

This recipe calls for equal amounts of ground pork and beef. Feel free to use any combination of ground meat. You even can use ground turkey, if you like. Just remember that ground turkey breast is much lower in fat than other ground meats and will produce a drier meatball.

TECHNIQUES

Browning the Meatballs

The light coating of flour will help create a thin crust around the meatballs when you sauté them in oil. Just make sure to coat them right before cooking, otherwise the meat will absorb the flour and you will not achieve the proper texture.

ADVANCE PREPARATION

This recipe can be made a day in advance and reheated.

MEATBALLS

3/4 pound ground beef

3/4 pound ground pork

2 large eggs

2 tablespoons dried oregano

2 teaspoons ground cumin

4 cloves garlic, finely chopped

2 teaspoons salt

1/4 teaspoon black pepper

About 1 cup all-purpose flour, to lightly coat the meatballs

1 tablespoon olive oil

SAUCE

1 tablespoon olive oil (optional)

1 onion, quartered

2 large tomatoes, cored and quartered

2 canned chipotles

2 tablespoons adobo from canned chipotles

1 1/2 tablespoons honey

1/2 teaspoon salt, plus more as needed

1 cup chicken broth

GARNISH

Mexican crema, homemade (page 102) or store-bought

Fresh cilantro sprigs

Fried tortilla strips or chips

FORM THE MEATBALLS

Combine the ground meats in a mixing bowl. Add the eggs, oregano, cumin, garlic, salt, and pepper. Using your hands, mix the ingredients until well incorporated.

Form the meatballs by placing 1 tablespoon of meat in the palms of your hand and moving both hands together in a circular motion to form a 1-inch ball. Set aside and repeat until all of the meat is used.

Put the flour on a dish. Cover the meatballs with a light dusting of flour by rolling them in the flour and shaking off the excess. Set aside.

BROWN THE MEATBALLS

Heat the olive oil in a saucepan over medium-high heat. When the oil is hot, add the meatballs in small batches, being careful not to crowd the pan because this will cause the meatballs to steam and not brown. You are looking to brown the meatballs on all sides but not cook them through. The meatballs will finish cooking in the sauce. Place the browned meatballs on a dish and set aside.

Use this same pan—with all the meat bits and rendered fat—to cook the sauce. Make sure there is about 1 tablespoon of oil left in the pan. If there is not, add more olive oil.

PUREE AND COOK THE SAUCE

Combine the onion, tomatoes, chipotles, adobo sauce, honey, and salt in a blender and puree until smooth.

Place the sauté pan used to brown the meatballs over medium-high heat and add the pureed sauce. Be careful because the sauce most likely will splatter. Cook the sauce for 2 minutes, then add the chicken broth. Reduce the heat to a simmer and continue cooking, uncovered, for 5 minutes.

SIMMER THE MEATBALLS

Taste the sauce for seasoning and adjust if necessary. Add the meatballs and cook for 10 minutes. The meatballs can sit in the sauce until you are ready to serve them. Just turn off the heat and cover the pan.

GARNISH AND SERVE

Because the sauce may be a bit spicy for some, serve the meatballs with Homemade Mexican Crema to tame the heat. Garnish with sprigs of cilantro and crispy strips of tortilla.

1. Assemble all of the meatball ingredients, then combine until well incorporated.

2. Form the meatballs by placing a portion of the meat mixture on the palm of your hand then rolling the mixture between both hands in a circular motion.

3. Serve the cooked meatballs over crema and garnish with extra sauce and fresh cilantro.

Sautéed Steak a la Mexicana

This classic dish proudly displays the colors of the Mexican flag, which is most likely why it's referred to as "belonging to Mexico" (a la Mexicana). It's also where the fajita probably got its start. A quick sauté of traditional ingredients—tomato, onion, and chiles—shows how delicious and simple Mexican food can be. **SERVES 4**

COOKING NOTES

INGREDIENTS

Flat Iron Steak

This cut, also known as top blade steak, is gaining popularity because it is incredibly flavorful, tender, and affordable. It looks like a tough cut, but don't be fooled by appearance. It sautés unbelievably well. If you can't find flat iron steak, substitute skirt steak or sirloin.

Poblano Chiles

Don't be tempted to substitute green bell pepper for the poblano chile. The flavor, not to mention the appearance, will not be the same. Poblanos contribute a depth of flavor and a slight amount of heat to the dish that bell peppers just don't deliver. Poblanos also retain an attractive deep green color that bell peppers don't. If you can't find poblanos, use a fresh jalapeño in place of the two roasted poblanos.

TECHNIQUES

Seeding Tomatoes

Cut the tomato in quarters lengthwise and then slice off the seedy pulp. Plum tomatoes are best for this recipe because they contain fewer seeds and less pulp than the round varieties.

ADVANCE PREPARATION

The poblano can be roasted, peeled, and sliced in advance.

2 poblano chiles
1 pound flat iron steak (top blade steak), sliced into $^1/_2$-inch-thick strips
Salt and black pepper
2 limes
$^1/_4$ cup olive oil
1 garlic clove, halved
1 onion, sliced
2 plum tomatoes, cored, seeded, and sliced into strips

ROAST AND PREPARE POBLANOS

Over an open flame of a gas stove or barbeque grill or in a dry cast-iron or nonstick skillet over high heat, roast the chiles until they are charred on all sides. This will take a few minutes over an open flame and about 10 minutes in a skillet.

Remove the chiles from the heat and seal in a plastic bag for 5 minutes. This will create steam and allow the skins to separate from the flesh. If you don't have a plastic bag, place the chiles in a bowl and cover tightly with aluminum foil or plastic wrap.

Peel away the skins. Cut off the stem end and remove the seeds and veins from the interior. Slice into $^1/_2$-inch-wide strips.

MARINATE THE BEEF

Lay the strips of beef flat on a platter or on a piece of aluminum foil laid on top of the counter. Season generously with salt and pepper and squeeze the juice of half a lime over it. Repeat with the other side. Allow to marinate while you work on the onions.

SWEAT THE ONIONS

Place a large sauté pan (large enough to eventually hold all the vegetables and the beef) over medium heat. Add 2 tablespoons of the oil along with the garlic while the pan heats up. When the garlic starts to sizzle, remove and discard it (you will have infused the oil with the garlic flavor). Add the onion, season with salt and pepper, and allow to slowly cook over medium heat for 10 minutes, stirring the onions every few minutes. As soon as they become limp and transparent, remove the onions from the pan and place them on a dish.

SAUTÉ THE BEEF

Add the remaining 2 tablespoons oil to the pan and increase the heat to high. As soon as the oil is hot, add the beef, making sure to not stack the strips on top of each other (this will steam—not sear—them). Sauté the beef until the strips reach your desired doneness, 7 to 8 minutes.

Add the onions, tomatoes, and roasted poblano strips to the pan and sauté for another 2 minutes. Check for seasoning, and add more salt and pepper if needed.

GARNISH AND SERVE

Transfer the steak to a serving platter. Slice the remaining lime into wedges and serve with the steak.

1. Assemble all of your ingredients.

2. Pour the blended spice mixture over the ground meats.

3. Protect your hands with plastic gloves or bags, then mix the ingredients until they are well incorporated.

4. Place the mixture on a piece of parchment paper and shape into a log.

5. Wrap the parchment paper securely around the chorizo mixture and refrigerate overnight.

Mexican Chorizo

Mexican chorizo has a flavor all its own. It is not only easy to make, but its ingredients are also commonly found in your local supermarket. Unlike its Spanish cousin, this chorizo is not cured or smoked. And because most Mexican recipes call for the chorizo to be removed from its casing, stuffing it is not necessary. Just measure out the chorizo into small portions before storing, and it is ready whenever you are. **MAKES 5 CUPS**

COOKING NOTES

TECHNIQUES

Mixing the Meat

The best way to mix the meat is with your hands. However, you will want to use plastic gloves—or create makeshift ones by putting your hands in plastic bags. That way you won't smell like chorizo for days.

ADVANCE PREPARATION

The chorizo mixture must be made a day before it is to be used and left in the refrigerator overnight. Do not skip this step because it is an important and necessary one to properly blend and develop all the flavors.

Once the chorizo has rested overnight, it can stay in the refrigerator for 2 days or be frozen for up to 3 months in 1-cup or $1/2$-cup portions in individual sealable plastic bags. Frozen chorizo should be thawed in the refrigerator. Always make sure the meat is cooked through before serving.

SERVING SUGGESTIONS

Mexican chorizo is as much a condiment as it is a stand-alone meat. Use the chorizo as a filling for a tamal or an omelet or use it to flavor stews and soups. In this book, you will find it in the Shredded Pork Stew with Smoky Chipotle Tomato Sauce (page 74) and the Chile, Cheese & Chorizo Melt (page 13).

2 cloves garlic

1 tablespoon salt

$1/2$ cup red wine vinegar

$1/2$ teaspoon black pepper

1 tablespoon dried oregano

1 teaspoon sugar

3 tablespoons ancho chile powder

1 canned chipotle

1 tablespoon adobo sauce from canned chipotle

2 tablespoons water

1 pound lean ground beef

1 pound ground pork

PUREE THE SPICE MIXTURE

Combine the garlic, salt, vinegar, black pepper, oregano, sugar, ancho chile powder, chipotle, adobo sauce, and water in a blender. Puree until you have a smooth paste.

BLEND THE GROUND MEATS

Put both ground meats in a bowl and pour in the pureed spice mixture. Using your hands, work the puree into the meats until well incorporated. Place the mixture on a piece of parchment paper and shape into a log. Wrap the parchment securely around the chorizo twisting the ends closed, and refrigerate overnight. Alternatively, transfer the mixture to a large resealable plastic bag and refrigerate overnight.

STORE THE CHORIZO

If you are planning to use the chorizo within 2 days, leave it in the refrigerator. Otherwise divide the chorizo in $1/2$-cup or 1-cup portions and place in individual airtight freezer bags and store in the freezer. The chorizo can be kept frozen for up to 3 months.

Seared Shredded Beef with Roasted Tomato Salsa

If I had to come up with two words to describe this dish, they would be "tangy" and "tasty." Onions, lime juice, and roasted tomato are all mixed in with flank steak, which is seared to a crispy and juicy finish. While the dish is made entirely on the stovetop, you'd swear a grill was involved. This is another great option for entertaining because most of the recipe can be done a day in advance. **SERVES 6**

2 pounds flank steak, cut into 4 pieces
2 onions, 1 quartered and 1 sliced
$1/3$ cup olive oil
Juice of 4 limes (about 4 tablespoons)
Salt and black pepper
1 pound large tomatoes, cored
1 jalapeño, stem removed
1 onion, halved
2 tablespoons lightly packed cilantro leaves
Salt and black pepper
1 lime, cut into wedges

BOIL AND SHRED THE FLANK STEAK

Combine the flank steak and quartered onion in a saucepan and fill with enough water to cover the meat. Bring to a boil, then decrease the heat to a simmer, leaving the pan uncovered. Continue simmering for 20 minutes, or until the beef is cooked through to a medium doneness (you can test the meat by tearing a piece open and making sure that the interior is pink in color). Remove the meat from the pan and place on a dish until it's cool enough to handle. Shred the beef and put in a bowl.

COOKING NOTES
TECHNIQUES

Shredding Beef

Flank steak is one of the easiest cuts to shred by hand since the muscle is made up of long stringy fibers. After the beef has been cooked, put it on a plate until it is cool enough to handle. Using your hands, shred the beef by pulling apart the fibers. You can decide how thick you want the beef shreds to be—I prefer them on the thin side.

ADVANCE PREPARATION

The recipe can be made up to the point of marinating the beef a day in advance. You can also sear the beef up to $1^{1}/2$ hours in advance of serving and hold it in a warm (250°F) oven.

MARINATE THE SHREDDED BEEF

Add the olive oil, sliced onion, lime juice, and salt and pepper to taste to the shredded beef and toss well. Cover the bowl with plastic wrap and marinate in the refrigerator for about 20 minutes, or overnight.

MAKE THE SALSA

Put a large nonstick skillet over medium heat and add the tomatoes, jalapeño, and onion in one layer. Allow the vegetables to cook through and char on all sides (this will intensify the flavors and bring out the sweetness). Resist the temptation to increase the heat to high, which will burn, not char, the vegetables.

Combine the charred vegetables (leave the skin on) and the cilantro in a food processor and pulse until it has the consistency of a chunky sauce. Season with salt and pepper and pour into a small serving bowl.

SEAR THE SHREDDED BEEF

Take the unwashed skillet used to char the vegetables and place it over medium-high heat. Toss the marinated beef and add about half of it to the skillet (you do not need to add more oil as the marinade has enough). You want to sear and crisp up the beef, not steam it, so avoid adding too much meat at one time. Do not touch the beef for 2 minutes. Allow the bottom layer of the flank steak to become golden brown and the onions to caramelize. Stir the mixture well, distribute it evenly in the skillet a second time, and allow it to sit another 2 minutes undisturbed. Transfer to a plate and repeat with the remaining beef.

SERVE AND GARNISH

Put the shredded beef on a platter and garnish with lime wedges and cilantro sprigs. Serve with the salsa.

Grilled Sirloin
with Creamy Salsa Verde

Simply grilled meat is a universal crowd-pleaser. Mexicans spend long weekend afternoons slowly grilling meat, which they serve with radish wedges, avocado slices, and various table sauces. This recipe puts it all together for you. So the next time you find yourself grilling, include this smooth salsa made with avocado and tomatillos, which is so velvety no one will believe you when you tell them it is made without cream. **SERVES 4**

COOKING NOTES
INGREDIENTS

Sirloin

Sirloin is a great grilling steak, but feel free to use your favorite cut.

Slicing an Avocado

The easiest way to slice an avocado is in its skin. But first you have to slice it in half. Cut the avocado in half by slicing halfway into it with a large knife and once you hit the seed in the center, move your knife along its perimeter. Twist the avocado open by gently pulling on each half.

Remove the seed by tapping the seed with the sharp edge of your knife, causing the knife to become wedged into the seed. Twist the knife a bit to dislodge the seed. Discard.

Finally, slice the avocado by taking the tip of your knife and drawing straight lines across the avocado flesh. Keep in mind, the tighter the lines, the thinner the slice. Make sure the tip of the knife reaches the skin of the avocado. Use a spoon to scoop out the sliced avocado.

TECHNIQUES

Indoor Grilling

Grill pans offer a good alternative to grilling outdoors. If you do not have one, just sear the meat in a cast-iron or stainless steel pan.

ADVANCE PREPARATION

The sauce can be made up to a day in advance. The avocado will not turn the sauce brown because the tomatillos are acidic enough to prevent the discoloration.

$^1/_2$ pound (about 5) tomatillos, husks and stems removed (see Cooking Notes, page 95)

1 jalapeño, stemmed

$^1/_2$ cup lightly packed cilantro, tender stems and leaves, plus sprigs for garnish

1 clove garlic

2 large green onions or scallions, tops and roots trimmed

$^1/_4$ teaspoon salt, plus more to taste

1 tablespoon water

1 avocado, pitted

4 sirloin steaks

Black pepper

2 radishes, quartered

Juice of 1 lime

PREPARE THE CREAMY SALSA VERDE

Combine the tomatillos, jalapeño, cilantro, garlic, green onions, salt, water, and half of the avocado in a blender or food processor. Puree until smooth. Check for seasoning and adjust if necessary.

GRILL THE BEEF

Preheat a grill to medium-high.

Season the meat generously with salt and pepper. Brush the grill grates with some olive oil. (If using a grill pan, place over high heat and add 2 tablespoons of olive oil.) Grill the meat to your desired doneness, about 4 minutes per side for medium. Remove from the heat and allow to rest for 5 minutes.

PREPARE THE SIDE SALAD AND SERVE

Slice the other half of the avocado (see Cooking Notes) and place it on a platter along with the radish wedges. Sprinkle with lime juice and season with salt and pepper. Garnish with sprigs of cilantro.

Serve the steaks accompanied by the salsa verde and the avocado and radish salad.

Shredded Pork Stew with Smoky Chipotle Tomato Sauce

This is an incredibly satisfying stew that gets better as it ages, so think about making extra to keep as leftovers. The smoky chipotles add a depth of flavor along with a spicy heat. To tame the heat, you can reduce the number of chipotles or serve the stew with Mexican crema. **SERVES 6**

1 pound pork shoulder

2 bay leaves

3 cloves garlic, 2 crushed and 1 chopped

2 tablespoons olive oil

1 pound fresh Mexican chorizo, homemade (page 71), or store-bought, casing removed

1 onion, sliced

1 teaspoon salt

1 1/2 pounds (about 7) plum tomatoes, halved lengthwise, cored, and sliced

2 canned chipotle chiles, chopped

1/4 cup adobo sauce from canned chipotles

1/2 teaspoon dried oregano

2 sprigs fresh thyme, leaves removed from stem

2 sprigs fresh marjoram, leaves removed from stem

GARNISH

6 sprigs cilantro

Tortilla chips

Mexican crema, homemade (page 102) or store-bought

COOKING NOTES

INGREDIENTS

Pork

You need a fatty cut of meat for this recipe, so if you cannot find shoulder, the only other cut to use is pork butt. A lean cut will result in tough and dry pork.

You can easily substitute beef flank steak for the pork. The beef only needs to be simmered for 30 minutes, but cooks the same as the pork after that.

Canned Chipotle Chiles

Look for the chipotles that are packed in adobo sauce. Chipotles are smoked jalapeños and have the heat of a jalapeño, but you can remove the seeds found in the chile if you want to reduce the heat.

ADVANCE PREPARATION

This dish improves with age as its flavors really blend. You can make this recipe up to 1 day in advance.

PREPARE THE MEAT

Put the pork in a saucepan and fill with enough water to cover the meat by 1 inch. Add the bay leaves and crushed garlic. Bring to a boil and skim off the grayish foam that rises to the top during the first few minutes. Decrease the heat to a simmer and cook for 45 minutes, partially covered, or until the pork is tender.

Allow the pork to cool in the stock, then drain, reserving 1 cup of the stock. Shred the pork by pulling apart the fibers with your fingers. Set aside.

PREPARE THE CHORIZO

Heat 1 tablespoon of the olive oil in a saucepan over medium heat. Add the chorizo to the pan and cook, breaking it apart as you stir, until it achieves a golden brown color and begins to render its fat. (Don't worry if some of the chorizo sticks to the bottom of the pan.) Using a slotted spoon, remove the chorizo from the pan and set it aside.

BROWN THE MAIN INGREDIENTS

Add the remaining 1 tablespoon olive oil to the unwashed pan and set it over medium heat. Add the onion and remaining chopped garlic and sauté until the onion begins to get limp and translucent, 3 minutes. Add the shredded pork, season with the salt, and continue sautéing for 3 more minutes. Deglaze the pan by pouring in a couple of tablespoons of the reserved pork stock and scraping the bottom of the pan with a heatproof silicone spatula.

FINISH THE STEW

Add the chorizo, tomatoes, chipotles, adobo from canned chipotles, oregano, thyme leaves, and marjoram leaves to the pan. Stir well and simmer for 5 minutes. Pour in the remaining reserved pork stock and continue simmering, uncovered, for 25 minutes.

GARNISH AND SERVE

Pour the finished stew into a large shallow bowl and garnish sprigs of cilantro. Serve with tortilla chips and Mexican crema.

Vegetables, Rice & Beans

Black Beans

Nothing compares to the flavor of homemade black beans. If you have never bothered making them, opting instead for the canned variety, you are in for a pleasant awakening! Luscious and meaty, they are so versatile that they can become a meal on their own when served with rice. The hardest part to making black beans is remembering to soak them overnight and then scheduling a couple of hours at home to cook them. But because they freeze and reheat so nicely, you can make a large batch and always have some on hand. **SERVES 8 TO 10**

1 pound dried black beans

8 cups water

$1/2$ cup olive oil

1 onion, chopped

4 cloves garlic, finely chopped

4 teaspoons salt, plus more as needed

1 teaspoon black pepper, plus more as needed

$1/2$ teaspoon dried oregano

1 bay leaf

COOKING NOTES

TECHNIQUES

Soaking the Beans

Overnight Soak: The only hard part is remembering to do it. Just combine the dried beans and water in a saucepan, cover, and let sit overnight at room temperature.

Quick Soak: If you forget to soak your beans overnight or if you decide at the last minute to make them, bring a covered pot filled with the beans and water to a boil, remove from the heat, and let sit for 3 hours. Then continue with the recipe from the "Simmer the Beans" point.

INGREDIENTS

Salt

It is important not to add salt to the beans until they have softened. Adding salt too early in the process will increase the time it takes for the beans to tenderize. This will substantially add to the cooking time.

ADVANCE PREPARATION

The beans can be made up to 3 days in advance and will keep for up to a week in the refrigerator. You can also freeze the beans after they have been cooked. Frozen beans will keep for up to 2 months in an airtight container. Just remember to freeze in small useable portions; a large tub of beans will take a long time to defrost.

SOAK THE BEANS

Rinse the dried beans with water and pick through them, removing any pebbles or debris you find.

Combine the beans and the water in a large saucepan, cover with a lid, and allow to sit at room temperature for 8 hours, or overnight. (Refer to Techniques for a quick-soak method.)

SIMMER THE BEANS

Place the saucepan with the soaked beans and water over medium heat. Simmer the beans, uncovered, for 1 hour, or until tender.

CHECK FOR TENDERNESS

Test one bean by pinching it between your fingers. If it easily caves to pressure, the beans are ready. If the beans are still tough, continue simmering until they soften. This requires some judgement on your part; you ultimately decide how soft you want the beans to be. If you continue cooking, there is no need to add more liquid, just make sure to stir the pot often.

SAUTÉ THE ONION AND GARLIC MIXTURE

Once the beans are tender, sauté the onion and garlic. Heat the olive oil in a skillet over medium-low heat. Add the onion and garlic and cook them slowly over low heat, for about 10 minutes. You want to sweat the vegetables—not brown them. When ready they will be very soft and translucent.

ADD THE ONION MIXTURE TO THE BEANS

To the simmering beans, add the onion mixture along with the salt, pepper, oregano, and bay leaf. Mix well and simmer, uncovered, for another 45 minutes. At this point, the liquid in the pan should barely be skimming the top layer of beans.

ADJUST SEASONING AND SERVE

Before serving, check for seasoning and add salt and pepper as needed.

Cilantro Rice

This is the perfect side dish on so many levels. It brings color and flavor to the table without competing with other dishes, and adds brightness to the table with the fresh cilantro garnish. Once you realize how easy the rice is to make and how well it reheats (allowing you to make it ahead of time), you will find yourself making it over and over again. **SERVES 6**

1 cup lightly packed cilantro, tender stems and leaves, plus sprigs for garnish

1 onion, quartered

2 cloves garlic

1 poblano chile, stemmed and seeded

2 cups chicken broth

2 tablespoons olive oil

1 1/2 cups long-grain rice

1 teaspoon salt

COOKING NOTES

INGREDIENTS

Poblano Chile

If you can't find a poblano chile, you can substitute a seeded jalapeño (it will add more heat) or just eliminate it from the recipe.

TECHNIQUES

Oven-Rice Cooking

Rice cooks just as well in the oven as it does on the stovetop. Cooking in the oven is a good option if you are short on stove space or if you are making the rice in advance and want to keep it warm in the oven.

Preheat the oven to 350°F and follow the recipe up to the point where you add the chicken broth and salt. Cover the pan and place it in the oven for 30 minutes. After the rice is cooked, remove the pan from the oven and let sit for 5 minutes before fluffing the rice with a fork.

If you are not going to serve the rice right away, lower the oven temperature to 200°F. After fluffing the rice with a fork, cover the pan and return it to the oven. The rice can be left warming for up to 2 hours.

ADVANCE PREPARATION

The rice can be made in advance—or kept as leftovers—and reheated in the microwave. Just place the rice in a shallow bowl, sprinkle it lightly with water, and cook for 3 minutes, or until it is heated through.

PUREE THE VEGETABLES

Combine the cilantro, onion, garlic, poblano chile, and 2 tablespoons of the chicken broth in a blender. Puree until smooth and set aside.

SAUTÉ THE RICE

Heat the oil in a saucepan over medium heat. When the oil is hot, add the rice and stir to coat well. Sauté for about 1 minute, or until the rice begins to smell toasty.

Add the cilantro puree and stir until all the rice is evenly coated with the mixture. Pour in the remaining chicken broth and season with the salt.

SIMMER THE RICE

Bring the liquid to a simmer, cover the pan, and continue simmering for 30 minutes.

FLUFF AND SERVE

Remove the pan from the heat and let sit for 5 minutes before uncovering and fluffing the rice with a fork. Transfer to a serving dish and garnish by topping with sprigs of cilantro.

Charred Corn with Lime, Chile & Crema

Considered one of Mexico's most popular street foods, this is not only an easy side dish, it's a show-stopper! Ears of corn—with their husks pulled back—are slightly charred to bring out their sweetness. Served with Mexican crema, chile, and lime, it packs a flavorful punch! **SERVES 6**

6 fresh ears of corn, silks removed but husks left intact
2 limes, quartered
2 tablespoons cayenne pepper
1 cup Mexican crema, homemade (page 102) or
    store-bought
Salt

COOKING NOTES
INGREDIENTS

Corn

This recipe can be made with corn that has been husked, using aluminum foil as a substitute for the husk. Place an ear of corn in the center of a sheet of aluminum foil. Sprinkle with a small amount of water and wrap the foil around the corn. Cook as instructed in the recipe. To char the corn, simply remove and discard the foil.

TECHNIQUES

Removing Silks from Corn

The silks are the thin strings found inside the husk. Since they are inedible, they need to be removed. To do so, gently pull back the husks halfway down the ear of corn and pull out the silks. It is fine if a few are left behind. Fold the husks back over the corn.

Making the Corn in the Oven

This recipe can be made easily in the oven. Soak the corn as instructed and preheat the oven to 400°F. Roast the corn on a baking sheet for 20 minutes. Then allow it to rest outside the oven for 5 minutes.

Cover all of the husks with aluminum foil (so that they do not burn) and char the corn in the oven under the broiler.

ADVANCE PREPARATION

The corn can be soaked and grilled or roasted a few hours ahead of time and charred before serving.

SOAK THE CORN

Place the corn in a large stockpot, bowl, or any container large enough to hold all the ears of corn and fill it with water. (The corn must be submerged under water so make sure your container is large enough.) If you don't have a sufficiently large container, use your kitchen sink.

Allow the corn to soak for 20 minutes. Remove from the container, shake off the excess water, and tightly squeeze the husks against the kernels of corn.

GRILL THE CORN

Heat an outdoor grill to medium-high. Place the corn on the rack and grill for 10 minutes. Turn the corn over and grill for another 10 minutes. Remove from the grill and let sit for 5 minutes.

PULL BACK THE HUSKS AND CHAR THE CORN

Take the grilled ears of corn and pull back the husks, exposing the kernels.

Place a sheet of aluminum foil on one side of the hot grill. Place the pulled back husks over the foil, allowing the exposed kernels to sit over the open grill. (This is done so the husks don't burn before the corn can char.)

Allow the kernels to char for about 4 minutes per side, or until they become dark and golden brown on all sides.

SERVE WITH GARNISHES

Brush or slather the corn with crema. I also like to dip lime wedges in cayenne pepper so that when they're squeezed over the corn, the heat and acid are evenly distributed. Do this by placing the cayenne pepper on a small dish and pressing one side of the lime wedge onto it. Make sure to leave a few wedges pepper-free for those who don't like it hot.

Surprisingly, if you use all of the condiments, the corn does not need salt. However, since that is a matter of taste, you may want to place some on the table.

Corn Tart

This is a great accompaniment to almost every recipe in this book because it offers a sweet counterpart to most of the spicy and tangy flavors found in other recipes. And because the ingredients needed are found in most pantries, the batter can be whipped up at a moment's time and left to bake unattended. **SERVES 6**

5 cups fresh corn kernels (about 8 ears fresh corn)
 or 5 cups frozen corn kernels, defrosted (see Cooking Notes, page 14)
2 tablespoons milk
4 large eggs, separated
4 tablespoons unsalted butter, melted
1 tablespoon cornstarch
1 teaspoon baking powder
1 1/2 teaspoons salt

COOKING NOTES

INGREDIENTS

Corn

Frozen corn works just as well as fresh corn and is preferable during the winter when corn is not in season. If you are using frozen corn, measure the amount needed before defrosting.

TECHNIQUES

Pureeing Corn

A food processor is the best equipment to use for this. You can put all the ingredients in at once and let it puree. A blender can also work; however, you may have to puree the corn in batches and scrape down the mixture with a rubber spatula.

ADVANCE PREPARATION

This dish is best eaten soon after it has come out of the oven. However, you can serve it at room temperature after it has sat for an hour or so.

SERVING SUGGESTIONS

While this recipe calls for a 9-inch square or round baking dish, you can go the extra mile and make individual tarts in 6-ounce ramekins. Reduce the baking time to 30 minutes. The individual tarts are ready when a skewer inserted into the center comes out clean.

PREHEAT THE OVEN AND PREPARE THE PAN
Preheat the oven to 350°F. Grease a 9-inch square or round baking dish with butter. Set aside.

PUREE THE CORN
Combine the corn and the milk in a food processor and puree until the corn is well blended. The result will be a mixture with a rough consistency.

PREPARE THE EGGS
Put the egg yolks in a large mixing bowl and, using a rubber spatula, mix until well blended. Add the pureed corn mixture, melted butter, cornstarch, baking powder, and salt. Mix well.

Put the egg whites in a bowl. Using an electric hand-mixer, beat until stiff peaks form. Using the same rubber spatula, stir one-quarter of the beaten egg whites into the corn mixture. Carefully fold in the remaining egg whites.

BAKE
Pour the corn mixture into the prepared baking dish and bake for 1 hour. The tart is ready when a skewer inserted in its center comes out clean and the top is golden brown.

SERVE
Because the texture of the tart is similar to that of a soufflé, the best way to serve it is to scoop it out of the pan with a large spoon.

Mexican Red Rice

Rice usually serves as a blank canvas for the rest of the dish. But not this one! This traditional rice imparts a beautiful red hue as well as a flavorful punch. Feel free to experiment with the quantity and variety of fresh chiles in the recipe—using or removing the seeds to control the heat as you see fit. **SERVES 6**

2 large tomatoes, cored and quartered

1 onion, quartered

2 cloves garlic

1 jalapeño, stemmed

3 tablespoons olive oil

2 cups long-grain white rice

1¹/₂ cups chicken broth or water

2 teaspoons salt

COOKING NOTES

INGREDIENTS

Chicken Broth versus Water

While its fine to use either ingredient, the chicken broth will impart a richer flavor to the rice. Vegetable broth is another good option.

TECHNIQUES

Imparting the Red Color

The pureed tomatoes will give the rice its red color. Therefore, it is important to use the ripest and reddest tomatoes you can find.

ADVANCE PREPARATION

Rice is always best eaten the day it is made. However, any leftovers can be kept in the refrigerator and reheated in the microwave. Just sprinkle a bit of water over the rice before reheating to make sure it doesn't dry out too much.

PUREE THE VEGETABLES

Combine the tomatoes, onion, garlic, and jalapeño in a blender and puree until smooth. You may need to poke the mixture with the handle of a wooden spoon while the blender is turned off to get the puree going.

SAUTÉ THE RICE AND VEGETABLE PUREE

Heat the oil in a saucepan over medium-high heat. When the oil is hot, add the rice and stir for 2 minutes or until the rice is completely coated in oil and it begins to release a toasty aroma.

Add the vegetable puree, taking care not to get splattered by the mixture, which will steam as soon as it hits the pan. Stir until the puree and rice are well blended.

SIMMER THE RICE

Add the chicken broth along with the salt and bring to a simmer. Cover and continue to simmer for 30 minutes.

FLUFF AND SERVE

Remove the pan from the heat and allow to sit, covered, for 5 minutes before fluffing up with a fork. Transfer to a serving dish and serve.

Refried Beans

Keep in mind that your refried beans are only as good as the beans with which you begin. If you want really flavorful refried beans, you must start with homemade beans, such as the recipe I provide on page 78. Those make especially good refried beans since they have a good amount of broth, which reduces during cooking and provides an incredible depth of flavor. In a bind, you can use canned beans—just keep in mind that you will not achieve the same intensity of flavor. **SERVES 8**

6 strips bacon, chopped

1 small onion, chopped

3 cups homemade black beans with their broth (page 78)

1/4 cup queso fresco or feta cheese, crumbled

COOKING NOTES

INGREDIENTS

Bacon Drippings versus Lard

One thing is for sure: refried beans should be made with an animal fat. Purists will only use lard when making these beans, but I find it is best to use bacon drippings unless you can get freshly rendered lard (the refrigerated kind). A benefit of bacon is the crispy bacon nuggets that are left over, which you can use as a sort of chicharrón (crackling).

TECHNIQUES

Making Bacon Drippings

Don't be tempted to render bacon fat over high heat. Make sure you set the heat no higher than medium-high. Animal fats tend to have low smoking points (they burn at low temperatures), which can lead to an undesirable dark color and off-flavors.

ADVANCE PREPARATION

This recipe can be made a couple of days in advance. Store the crispy bacon in an airtight container in the refrigerator.

RENDER THE BACON FAT

Place a skillet over medium-high heat and add the bacon. Allow the bacon to cook slowly and melt its fat. As the bacon gets crispy, remove with a slotted spoon and drain on a paper towel. You can serve the bacon with the beans, or save them for another use.

SAUTÉ THE ONION

Keeping the skillet on the stove, decrease the heat to medium, and add the onion. Cook the onion slowly until soft and translucent, about 6 minutes. (The bacon fat can burn easily so make sure you do not increase the heat too high.)

MASH THE BEANS

Once the onions are soft, add half of the beans with their broth to the pan and stir to combine well. Using a potato masher or a fork, mash the beans until most of them are crushed.

Add the remaining beans with their broth and continue mashing until you achieve the consistency of a coarse puree. Stir to blend the mixture well.

Continue cooking over medium heat until any liquid that remains has been absorbed and the mashed bean mixture is creamy. Be careful not to burn the beans because that results in a bitter flavor.

GARNISH AND SERVE

Transfer the refried beans to a serving bowl and top with crumbles of queso fresco and crispy bacon.

Mushroom Quesadilla

These quesadillas are a great meatless option for a menu. Hearty and satisfying, the sautéed mushrooms are as delicious on their own as they are stuffed in the tortillas. And if you feel like changing it up a bit, experiment with different varieties of mushrooms. **MAKES 12 QUESADILLAS**

$^1/_4$ cup olive oil, plus more for searing

1 small onion, sliced

1 jalapeño, stemmed and chopped

10 ounces cremini mushrooms or any other variety, stems removed, caps sliced

1 teaspoon salt

Juice of 1 lime

12 (9-inch) flour tortillas

$1^1/_2$ cups Monterey Jack cheese, shredded

Mexican crema, homemade (page 102) or store-bought

Fresh Tomato Salsa (page 96)

Sprigs of cilantro, for garnish

COOKING NOTES

INGREDIENTS

Mushrooms

Although I make these quesadillas with cremini mushrooms, the traditional choice is white button mushrooms. However, feel free to experiment with different varieties and combinations of mushrooms.

TECHNIQUES

Heating the Quesadillas

Quesadillas should have a crisp crust, which is only achieved by heating the tortillas with a bit of oil. Make sure the pan is hot and has a nice coating of oil so that you are able to develop a golden brown crust.

ADVANCE PREPARATION

You can prepare the mushroom filling ahead of time—up to a day in advance. However, the quesadillas should be made right before serving.

SERVING SUGGESTION

These quesadillas are so versatile they can be served as an appetizer, main course, or side dish. They also make great hors d'oeuvres when cut into small wedges.

MAKE THE MUSHROOM FILLING

Heat 1 tablespoon of the oil in a large nonstick skillet over medium heat. Once the oil is hot, add the onion and jalapeño and sauté until the vegetables begin to soften, about 2 minutes.

Add the mushrooms, salt, and the lime juice. Increase the heat to medium-high and sauté for about 5 minutes, or until all of the liquid released by the mushrooms has evaporated. Transfer the mushroom mixture to a plate and set aside.

STUFF AND HEAT THE TORTILLAS

Return the same pan used to sauté the mushrooms, with whatever oil was left behind, to the stove and place over medium-high heat. Add 1 tablespoon of the oil and heat for 1 minute.

Place 2 tablespoons of the shredded cheese on the bottom half of each tortilla and top with 2 tablespoons of the mushroom mixture. Fold the tortilla over creating a half moon.

Place as many tortillas as will fit comfortably in the pan. Allow the quesadillas to sear for 1 minute, flip over, and sear for another minute. Remove from the pan and place on a serving platter. Repeat with the remaining ingredients, adding more oil to the skillet as needed.

GARNISH AND SERVE

Serve the quesadillas warm, accompanied by Mexican crema and tomato salsa. Garnish with sprigs of cilantro.

Roasted Chiles, Onions & Tomatoes

Roasting—or rather toasting—vegetables is one of the most important techniques in Mexican cooking. Because the roasting is done on the stovetop and not in the oven where the vegetables can steam, the flavors developed are very deep. Make sure to include some charred pieces of vegetable skin—they will add an incredible smoky flavor to your recipes. **MAKES ABOUT 4 CUPS**

COOKING NOTES
INGREDIENTS

Chiles

This technique can be used with almost every type of fresh chile. Poblanos are the traditional choice for roasting, but feel free to use jalapeños (which are spicier) and even green bell peppers, if you cannot find any other type.

Tomatoes

Roasting tomatoes really brings out their sweet flavor and adds a deeper dimension to any recipe in which they are used. This is true for all varieties of tomatoes—large, small, yellow, red. So try roasting a variety of colors and sizes, chopping them up, and tossing with oil and lime for an unexpected salad.

ADVANCE PREPARATION

Vegetables can be roasted ahead and kept in an airtight container in the refrigerator for about 4 days.

2 poblano chiles

2 onions, excess papery skin removed, cut in half

2 round tomatoes

ROASTING CHILES

Over an open flame of a gas stove or barbeque grill or in a dry cast-iron or nonstick skillet over high heat, roast the chiles until they are charred on all sides. This will take a few minutes over an open flame and about 10 minutes in a skillet.

Remove the chiles from the heat and seal in a plastic bag for 5 minutes. This will create steam and allow the skins to separate from the flesh. If you don't have a plastic bag, place the chiles in a bowl and cover tightly with aluminum foil or plastic wrap.

Peel away the skins. Cut off the stem end and remove the seeds and veins from the interior. Slice into $1/2$-inch-wide strips.

ROASTING ONIONS AND TOMATOES

The vegetables can be cooked together or separately. Put the tomatoes and onion in a dry cast-iron or non-stick skillet over medium-high heat. Allow the vegetables to roast and char on all sides by rotating them and turning them over with a pair of tongs. When all sides are charred, remove from the heat; this should take approximately 10 minutes. Allow the vegetables to cool slightly, then peel off the blistered skin.

SERVE

While these roasted vegetables are often used as an ingredient in other recipes, they also make a great side dish. Just transfer them to a platter and serve.

Sauces, Condiments & Marinades

Achiote Marinade (Recado)

It's hard to put my finger on what it is about this marinade that makes it so good. It could be the earthiness of the annatto seeds, but it could also be the sweet tanginess from the vinegar, cumin, and orange juice. Whatever it is, you will love it on your chicken, fish, or pork, as much for its flavor as for the striking deep red color it will pass on. **MAKES ¹/₂ CUP**

COOKING NOTES
INGREDIENTS

Annato Seed

This seed, which is also called achiote, gives off a musky and earthy flavor. It comes from the annatto tree and is used for both its flavor and red coloring. It is fine to use annatto powder, but the ground seeds are a much better option. The seeds are rather hard to crush by hand. If you do not have a spice grinder, use your blender to create the powder.

TECHNIQUES

Making a Garlic Paste

When you crush salt into a peeled garlic clove, the garlic will let go of its moisture and turn into a paste. This technique somehow magically mellows out the pungent flavor of raw garlic.

While you can create the paste using a knife (continue chopping a peeled garlic clove over a small mound of salt until you achieve a paste), a mortar and pestle is the easiest and best way to make the paste.

ADVANCE PREPARATION

This marinade can be stored in an airtight container in the refrigerator for up to 1 week.

SERVING SUGGESTIONS

This marinade goes incredibly well with chicken, fish, and pork.

---

1 teaspoon salt

4 cloves garlic

2 tablespoons annatto seeds, ground

1 teaspoon ground cumin

2 teaspoons dried oregano

¹/₂ teaspoon black pepper

3 tablespoons red wine vinegar

3 tablespoons freshly squeezed orange juice

MAKE A GARLIC PASTE
Crush the salt into the garlic using a mortar and pestle until a paste forms.

MIX IN THE SPICES
Add the annatto seeds, cumin, oregano, and black pepper and mix well.

ADD THE LIQUID
Pour in the vinegar and orange juice and stir well.

LET SIT, THEN STORE
Allow the marinade to sit for 5 minutes before using. You will notice that the marinade will become thicker after it sits for a few minutes.

If you are not going to use it right away, transfer the marinade to an airtight container and refrigerate.

Chipotle Chile Sauce

This is an incredibly versatile sauce that you will refer to as your "special sauce." It is creamy, smoky, and a bit spicy, and goes just as well with chicken and seafood as it does with meat and pork. But don't limit yourself to its conventional uses. Spread it on sandwiches or use it as a dip for vegetables.

MAKES 1 CUP

COOKING NOTES

TECHNIQUES

If you don't have a food processor or blender, you can still make the sauce by finely chopping the chipotle chiles and combining them with the mayonnaise and crema.

ADVANCE PREPARATION

This sauce can be made well in advance and kept in an airtight container in the refrigerator for up to 2 weeks.

$^1/_2$ cup mayonnaise

$^1/_2$ cup Mexican crema, homemade (page 102) or store-bought

2 canned chipotle chiles

PUREE THE INGREDIENTS

Place all the ingredients in a food processor or blender and puree until smooth.

SERVE OR STORE

Transfer to a serving bowl if using right away, or transfer to an airtight container and refrigerate if storing.

Fresh Tomatillo Sauce

This has become my favorite sauce—for now. Its fresh flavor, vibrant color, and slight heat (which you can control with the amount of jalapeños you add) are the reasons why. And once you discover how easy it is to prepare and how long it keeps in the refrigerator, I don't doubt it will become a favorite of yours, too. **MAKES 2¹/₂ CUPS**

1 pound (about 9) tomatillos, husks removed, rinsed, and quartered

2 jalapeños, stemmed and halved

1 cup lightly packed fresh cilantro stems and leaves

1 clove garlic

¹/₂ onion

¹/₂ teaspoon salt

2 tablespoons water

PUREE THE INGREDIENTS

Combine all the ingredients in a blender and pulse a few times before blending the ingredients into a puree.

SERVE OR STORE

Transfer to a serving bowl if using right away, or transfer to an airtight container and refrigerate if storing.

Fresh Tomato Salsa

This recipe is commonly referred to as *Pico de Gallo* (rooster's beak). I suppose it is because the ingredients are all chopped up as if they were broken up by a bird's beak. It is one of my favorites since it is not only delicious but also low fuss. Don't worry about chopping the vegetables into uniform sizes or shapes and certainly don't feel compelled to measure any of the ingredients. This chunky sauce goes well with almost every Mexican dish and is the classic accompaniment to serve with tortilla chips. **MAKES 2 CUPS**

COOKING NOTES

INGREDIENTS

Tomatoes

While round red tomatoes are the typical choice, feel free to experiment with different colors and sizes. This recipe works well when using a combination of tomatoes.

ADVANCE PREPARATION

This sauce is best made a half hour before you plan to serve it. It can be made a few hours before, but it will begin to get too watery if left to sit longer than a couple of hours.

SERVING SUGGESTIONS

For the classic chips and salsa, serve this sauce with tortilla chips.

- 2 large tomatoes (about 1 pound), cored and chopped
- 2 tablespoons finely chopped red onion
- $1/4$ cup lightly packed cilantro leaves, chopped, plus extra sprig for garnish
- 1 jalapeño, stemmed and finely chopped
- Juice of 1 lime
- $1/2$ teaspoon salt, or to taste

COMBINE THE INGREDIENTS

Put all the ingredients in a bowl and mix well.

ADJUST THE SEASONING

Allow the sauce to sit for about 5 minutes. The tomatoes will begin to let go of their juices and the salsa will become more liquid. Taste again for seasoning and adjust if needed.

SERVE OR STORE

Transfer to a serving bowl if using right away and garnish with sprig of cilantro. To store, cover with plastic wrap and keep refrigerated.

FRESH TOMATILLO SAUCE

FRESH TOMATO SALSA

FRESH TOMATO SAUCE

Fresh Tomato Sauce

This uncooked tomato sauce is a staple in the Mexican kitchen and is often served in small bowls and placed on tables as a condiment. It is a simple sauce to prepare, just be careful not to overprocess because it's meant to be a rustic sauce with a coarse texture. **MAKES 2 CUPS**

COOKING NOTES

INGREDIENTS

Cilantro

There are times when you may want to pick cilantro leaves off their tender stems, but that is not necessary in this recipe since all of the ingredients are going to be pureed. In fact, cilantro stems are very flavorful and should be used whenever possible.

TECHNIQUES

Pureeing

In order to prevent the sauce from becoming frothy, make sure that the tomato is the last ingredient to be added to the blender. I also recommend pulsing, as opposed to continuous pureeing, for the same reason.

ADVANCE PREPARATION

This sauce can be made up to a day in advance. After 24 hours, the sauce will take on an acidic flavor.

$1/4$ medium red onion, quartered

1 large jalapeño, stemmed and quartered

$1/2$ cup lightly packed cilantro leaves and tender stems

Juice of 1 lime

1 teaspoon salt, plus more as needed

4 (about 1 pound) plum tomatoes, cored and quartered

PUREE THE INGREDIENTS

Combine all of the ingredients in the order given in a blender and pulse until pureed. You want the sauce to be a bit chunky, so make sure not to overprocess.

ADJUST SEASONING

Taste for seasoning and adjust if needed.

SERVE OR STORE

Transfer to a serving bowl if using right away, or transfer to an airtight container and refrigerate if storing.

Roasted Tomato Salsa

This recipe is an updated version of the classic cooked Mexican tomato sauce, which is made with vegetable purees and simmered on the stove. My version roasts the vegetables in the oven, allowing them to caramelize, before they are pureed. The result is a sauce with deep rich flavor and a hint of sweetness. If you don't like heat, make sure to remove the seeds from the jalapeño! **MAKES 1¼ CUPS**

COOKING NOTES

INGREDIENTS

Tomatoes

Even though I use cherry tomatoes in the recipe, any type of tomato would work well here. Just keep in mind that larger ones will take longer to roast. Also, the sweeter the tomato, the sweeter the salsa.

TECHNIQUES

Roasting

Roasting vegetables really brings out their natural flavors by doing two things: dehydrating them concentrates their flavors and caramelizing them brings out their sweetness.

In order to achieve this you need a hot oven and the vegetables need space. Do not overcrowd or stack your vegetables because that will cause them to steam and not roast.

ADVANCE PREPARATION

If placed in an airtight container, the salsa will keep in the refrigerator for up to 1 week.

2 cups cherry tomatoes, halved

1 jalapeño, stemmed and halved

1 small onion, peeled and quartered

2 cloves garlic, unpeeled

2 tablespoons olive oil

Salt and black pepper

¼ cup red wine vinegar

¼ cup water

ROAST THE VEGETABLES

Preheat the oven to 400°F. Line a baking sheet with parchment paper or aluminum foil.

Place all of the vegetables on the prepared baking sheet, cut side up. Depending on the size of your baking sheet, you may need to use two sheets. Drizzle the vegetables with oil and season generously with salt and pepper.

Roast for 40 minutes, or until the tomatoes are shriveled up and develop bits of deep brown spots of color.

PUREE THE VEGETABLES

Transfer all of the roasted vegetables to a blender and add the vinegar and water. Puree until smooth. Taste the salsa and adjust the seasoning, if necessary.

SERVE OR STORE

Transfer to a serving bowl if using right away, or transfer to an airtight container and refrigerate if storing.

Red Chile Paste (Mexican Adobo)

This is an incredibly flavorful paste that is simply made and keeps almost indefinitely in the refrigerator. It is also easily doubled, so you might as well make extra to rub on meats, chicken, and fish. (Finished sauce pictured on page 90.) **MAKES 1 CUP**

4 dried ancho chiles

4 cloves garlic, unpeeled, but excess paper removed

$1/8$ teaspoon ground cinnamon

1 bay leaf, crushed

$1/2$ teaspoon ground cumin

$1/2$ teaspoon ground black pepper

$1/2$ teaspoon dried oregano

1 teaspoon salt

$1/4$ cup red wine vinegar

COOKING NOTES
INGREDIENTS

Handling Chiles

If you have sensitive hands, you may want to wear rubber gloves when handling chiles. If you chose to work with them with bare hands, make sure to wash your hands well before touching your eyes or other sensitive skin.

TECHNIQUES

Roasting Chiles

Although you may not think it makes a difference, dry roasting or toasting dried chiles before rehydrating them adds an incredible richness to their flavor. However, you must be careful not to burn them, which will result in an undesirable bitter flavor.

Since the chiles are dark, you cannot rely on their color to tell you if they are ready. Instead pay attention to their aroma and texture. As soon as they begin to release their scent and become soft and pliable, they are ready.

ADVANCE PREPARATION

This paste can be made well in advance and kept in an airtight container in the refrigerator. It keeps almost indefinitely.

ROAST AND SOAK THE CHILES

Cut or tear the chiles into flat pieces and remove the seeds and veins. Heat a nonstick skillet over medium heat and roast the chiles on both sides until they begin to release their aroma and soften up a bit, about 1 minute.

Transfer to a blender and fill with boiling water. Allow the chiles to soak for 30 minutes, making sure to keep them submerged under water. (You may need to wedge the blender top into the opening to help keep the chiles under water.)

ROAST THE GARLIC

Return the same skillet used to toast the chiles to the stove and place over medium heat. Add the garlic and roast, turning often, until the skin blackens and the garlic begins to smell toasty, about 10 minutes. Remove from the heat and peel. Set aside.

PUREE THE MIXTURE

Pour the water out of the blender jar, leaving behind the rehydrated chiles. Add the garlic along with cinnamon, bay leaf, cumin, pepper, oregano, salt, and vinegar and puree until smooth. (You may need to pulse and scrape down the mixture a few times to get the puree started.)

SERVE OR STORE

Transfer to a serving bowl if using right away, or transfer to an airtight container and refrigerate if storing.

Homemade Mexican Crema

A staple on Mexican tables, do not confuse Mexican crema for sour cream. The flavor is more sour, and it's a bit saltier as well. In addition to providing flavor and texture to a dish, the cream also serves as a neutralizer for the heat of chiles. It is a good option to have around for those who don't like hot foods. **MAKES 2 CUPS**

1 cup sour cream
1 cup heavy cream
1 teaspoon salt

COOKING NOTES

ADVANCE PREPARATION

When purchasing sour cream, pay attention to the expiration date. The crema can be made and stored in an airtight container in the refrigerator for as long as the sour cream would last.

Bring the crema to room temperature before serving.

MIX
Combine all the ingredients in a bowl, cover with plastic wrap, and set it out at room temperature for 3 hours.

SERVE OR STORE
Transfer to a serving bowl if using right away, or transfer to an airtight container and refrigerate if storing.

Guacamole

When most people think Mexican food, they think of guacamole. It's become almost synonymous with Mexican cooking. Traditionally guacamole is made in a *molcajete:* a stone mortar and pestle, which crushes the aromatic vegetables, allowing all the flavors to come out and truly marry. I must admit guacamole does taste better when made in a *molcajete*, but don't worry if you don't have one. I have come up with a technique that produces a guacamole with as much flavor. **SERVES 4**

$^{1}/_{4}$ white onion, chopped (about $^{1}/_{4}$ cup)

1 jalapeño, stemmed and chopped

$^{1}/_{2}$ cup lightly packed cilantro leaves, chopped, plus a few sprigs for garnish

1 teaspoon salt, plus more as needed

3 Hass avocados

1 plum tomato, chopped

Juice of 1 lime

COOKING NOTES

VARIATIONS

There are as many versions of guacamole as there are guacamole eaters. This is a classic rendition, which you can leave as is or use as a base for creating your own. Try adding more tomato or substituting a red onion for the white one. It's really up to you.

ADVANCE PREPARATION

Although there are a number of techniques claiming to slow down the browning reaction avocados undergo, I never seem to have much luck with them. This is one of those recipes where you just have to make it soon before eating. It can sit for 1 hour if you place a piece of plastic wrap directly on the surface of the guacamole.

CREATE A BASE WITH ONION, CILANTRO, AND JALAPEÑO

Put the onion in a mound in the center of your cutting board. Top it with the jalapeño and then the cilantro. Sprinkle $^{1}/_{2}$ teaspoon of the salt on the vegetables. Using your chef's knife, chop and crush the vegetables until they are very finely chopped. The salt will cause some of the moisture to be drawn out from the vegetables, which will help to blend their flavors.

Transfer the vegetables to a large, shallow bowl.

SCOOP OUT AND MASH THE AVOCADO

Cut the avocado in half lengthwise and remove the seed. Using a spoon, scoop out all of the flesh and place it in the bowl with the vegetables.

A mortar or tart tamper is a great tool for this next step. If you don't have either, a dinner fork will do just fine.

Mash the avocado until you achieve the consistency you want. This part is entirely up to you. There are some people who like their guacamole chunky, while others prefer it smooth. I like is somewhere in the middle, where I can still see some chunks of avocado but most of it is well blended.

SEASON AND GARNISH

Add the tomato, lime juice, and remaining $^{1}/_{2}$ teaspoon salt to the guacamole and combine well. Taste for seasoning and adjust if needed.

Garnish with a few sprigs of cilantro.

Desserts

Dos Leches Flan

Flan is the quintessential Latin dessert. I love how using two different milks (literally, *dos leches*) produces a creamy, velvety custard. This rendition is not only smooth and delicious, it is incredibly simple. The only "complicated" step is making the caramel. But you will see that it really isn't difficult. Just do it once and I promise you will be a pro! **SERVES 8**

COOKING NOTES
TECHNIQUES

Making Caramel

Forget about what you have heard, caramel is easy to make and easy to clean up. You just have to have the right tools: a nonstick pan and a heatproof silicone spatula. Using any other material will make for a messy and long clean up.

Follow the instructions in the recipe and if the sugar clumps up, keep heating it until it melts.

Creating a Water Bath

I find the easiest and safest way to create an oven water bath is to place a deep pan in the oven, fill it with water, and allow it to heat up during the oven preheating time.

Cleaning the Pans

The nonstick skillet and silicone spatula will clean up quickly after they have been used. A little hot soapy water should be enough to get all the hardened caramel off.

The loaf pan is a different story. You will most likely end up with a hardened layer of caramel stuck to your pan. Soak the pan in hot soapy water overnight. The next day, pour out the water and pour in clean hot water. Any remaining caramel should just melt right off.

ADVANCE PREPARATION

The flan can be baked and left in its pan, unmolded, in the refrigerator for 2 days. After it has been unmolded, it will keep for another 3 days or so.

1 (12-ounce) can evaporated milk

1 (14-ounce) can sweetened condensed milk

1 1/4 cups water

6 large eggs, lightly beaten

1/8 teaspoon salt

1 teaspoon vanilla extract

1 cup sugar

PREHEAT THE OVEN AND PREPARE A WATER BATH

Preheat the oven to 350°F.

Place a rectangular cake pan or roasting pan into the oven and pour in enough water to come halfway up the sides of the pan. Leave the pan in the oven while it preheats.

MIX THE FLAN INGREDIENTS

In a mixing bowl, combine the evaporated milk, condensed milk, water, eggs, salt, and vanilla. Mix until everything is well blended.

MAKE THE CARAMEL

This is actually much easier than you think. Just make sure you have a nonstick skillet and a heat-proof silicone spatula. Place a nonstick skillet over medium-high heat, sprinkle the sugar evenly all over it, and cook. After about 5 minutes, you will see the sugar begin to melt. A few minutes after that, parts of the melted sugar will begin to turn a light brown color. If the sugar is melting unevenly, you can use your silicone spatula to stir it around a bit. If you do, the sugar will clump up a bit, and that is okay. The clumps will eventually melt down—just continue stirring.

Once all of the sugar has melted (and any clumps have disappeared), pour the caramel into a 9 by 5-inch loaf pan, preferably a nonstick one. As soon as you pour the caramel into the pan, it will begin to harden, which is okay.

POUR THE FLAN MIXTURE INTO THE PAN AND BAKE

Give the flan mixture a quick mix and pour it over the prepared caramel in the pan.

Place the pan in the center of the water bath. You may hear some crackling, which is the hardened caramel.

Bake for 1 hour, or until a cake tester, toothpick, or butter knife inserted in the center of the flan comes out clean. The center will still jiggle a bit.

Remove the loaf pan from the oven and allow to cool for 1 hour. If you are going to unmold the flan in the next hour, leave the water bath in the oven. (After cooling for 45 minutes, you can cover the flan with plastic wrap and place it in the refrigerator until you are ready to unmold it.)

UNMOLD AND SERVE

You need your water bath again. If you discarded the one used for baking, place enough hot water in a rectangular cake pan or roasting pan to come at least a quarter of the way up the sides of the pan.

Dip the loaf pan into the hot water and let it sit for a few minutes. You will hear cracking again, which is the caramel loosening up. Remove the loaf pan from the hot water and run a thin knife blade between the flan and the sides of the pan.

Invert a serving platter over the loaf pan and flip both over, dislodging the flan from the pan. The caramel will drip down onto the platter. (A good amount of caramel will have remained in its solid state in the pan, which is expected.)

Serve and enjoy!

Fresh Fruit Ice Trio: Lime, Watermelon & Pineapple

Street vendors throughout Mexico's beach towns sell cold fresh fruit served in a plastic bag with bits of ice in it to keep the fruit chilled. This dessert is a take on that, as well as a refreshing end to any meal. Feel free to experiment by pouring a bit of tequila over the ice to create an instant margarita.

SERVES 6

COOKING NOTES

TECHNIQUES

Making Simple Syrup

Simple syrup is the name given to sugar dissolved in water. It is not enough to just stir some sugar in water; it has to be lightly heated so that the sugar actually dissolves. This is done to avoid a gritty texture.

ADVANCE PREPARATION

This is definitely a recipe that must be prepared ahead of time because the ices need several hours to freeze properly. After the ices have been frozen, they can be scraped, placed in airtight containers, and frozen until needed—the texture will be fine. The frozen ices can be kept in the freezer for a few weeks.

If you are keeping your ices frozen, prevent the ice from absorbing flavors from the freezer by completely wrapping the storage containers with plastic wrap. This will ensure an airtight environment.

LIME

3/4 cup sugar

2 1/4 cups water

1/2 cup fresh lime juice (about 6 limes)

Finely grated zest of 3 limes

PREPARE A SIMPLE SYRUP

Combine the sugar and water in a saucepan set over medium heat. Stir until the sugar has completely dissolved. Remove from the heat and allow the syrup to cool.

ADD THE LIME JUICE AND FREEZE

Pour the simple syrup and lime juice in a 9 by 11-inch nonreactive baking pan and stir in the lime zest. Cover the pan with plastic wrap and place in the freezer.

After 1 hour, stir the mixture well, using a fork. Return to the freezer for another hour, then stir again. Allow the mixture to freeze for at least 6 hours or overnight (it is not necessary to continue stirring after you have done it twice).

SERVE

Remove the pan from the freezer and allow it to sit at room temperature for about 5 minutes. Using a fork, scrape the fruit ice and serve it in a small bowl.

continued on page 110

WATERMELON

1/4 cup sugar

2 cups water

4 cups chopped seedless watermelon
(about 3 pounds whole fruit), rind removed

Juice of 1 lime

PREPARE A SIMPLE SYRUP

Combine the sugar and water in a saucepan set over medium heat. Stir until the sugar has completely dissolved. Remove from the heat and allow the syrup to cool.

PUREE THE WATERMELON AND FREEZE

Puree the watermelon chunks (it is fine if small seeds are still attached) in a blender until smooth. Pour the simple syrup, lime juice, and watermelon puree in a 9 by 11-inch nonreactive baking pan and stir well. Cover the pan with plastic wrap and place in the freezer.

After 1 hour, stir the mixture well, using a fork. Return to the freezer for another hour, then stir again. This time allow the mixture to freeze for at least 6 hours or overnight (it is not necessary to continue stirring after you have done it twice).

SERVE

Remove the pan from the freezer and allow it to sit at room temperature for about 5 minutes. Using a fork, scrape the fruit ice and serve it in a small bowl.

PINEAPPLE

1/2 cup sugar

2 cups water

1 pineapple, peeled, cored, chopped (about 3 cups)

PREPARE A SIMPLE SYRUP

Combine the sugar and water in a saucepan set over medium heat. Stir until the sugar has completely dissolved. Remove from the heat and allow the syrup to cool.

PUREE THE PINEAPPLE AND FREEZE

Puree the pineapple chunks in a blender until smooth. Pour the simple syrup and pineapple puree in a 9 by 11-inch nonreactive baking pan and stir well. Cover the pan with plastic wrap and place in the freezer.

After 1 hour, stir the mixture well using a fork. Return to the freezer for another hour, then stir again. This time allow the mixture to freeze for at least 6 hours or overnight (it is not necessary to continue stirring after you have done it twice).

SERVE

Remove the pan from the freezer and allow it to sit at room temperature for about 5 minutes. Using a fork, scrape the fruit ice and serve it in a small bowl.

Caramelized Crepes Stuffed with Dulce de Leche

If you think of crepes as thin pancakes, you will realize how easy they are to make. This recipe flavors the crepe batter with cinnamon and vanilla, resulting in a speckled crepe that goes great with any sweet filling. While I stuff these solely with dulce de leche, feel free to add chopped fresh fruit, such as strawberries, bananas, or mango, to the filling or to add fruit on top. **SERVES 6**

CREPE BATTER

1 cup all-purpose flour

$^2/_3$ cup water

$^2/_3$ cup milk

3 large eggs

$^1/_4$ teaspoon salt

1 teaspoon vanilla extract

$^1/_2$ teaspoon ground cinnamon

2 tablespoons unsalted butter, melted

Butter, for the pan

1$^1/_2$ cups dulce de leche or caramel sauce

2 tablespoons granulated sugar

Confectioners' sugar, for garnish

COOKING NOTES
TECHNIQUES

Resting the Crepe Batter

The secret to a successful crepe batter is to allow it to rest for at least an hour after the batter has been mixed. This allows the starch in the flour to absorb the liquid in the batter, which improves the texture of the crepe.

Caramelizing the Crepes

While you can skip this step, it really adds to the texture of the dessert. The easiest and most efficient way to do this is with a small blowtorch that can be found at most kitchenware stores. If you do not have one, place the baking dish as close to your broiler as you can get it and allow your broiler to caramelize the sugar.

ADVANCE PREPARATION

You can make the crepes a few hours in advance and keep them wrapped in plastic at room temperature. They will hold at room temperature stuffed with the dulce de leche filling for another couple of hours. It is best to eat the crepes the day they are made.

PREPARE THE CREPE BATTER

Combine the flour, water, milk, eggs, salt, vanilla, and cinnamon in a blender and puree until smooth. You may need to scrape down the sides of the jar a few times. Add the melted butter and mix well.

Leave the batter in the blender jar and allow it to rest in the refrigerator for up to 1 hour.

MAKE THE CREPES

Place a nonstick skillet over medium heat and brush some melted butter on it. When the pan is hot, use a ladle to pour in about 3 tablespoons of the batter. To help create a thin crepe, tilt your pan in all directions so the batter covers most of the surface of the pan.

Allow the crepe to cook until the edges start turning golden brown, about 2 minutes. Use a wide spatula to turn the crepe over. (I agree with the adage that says your first crepe never comes out right and you get a free do-over. The first one just coats the pan with fat so the rest cook evenly and slide off easily.)

Place the crepe on a dish and cover it with plastic to keep moist. Repeat until you run out of batter. You should be able to make about 12 crepes.

STUFF AND CARAMELIZE THE CREPES

Rub some butter on the bottom of a 1-quart baking dish (the shape doesn't matter) and set aside.

Working with one crepe at a time, place 2 tablespoons of dulce de leche in the center and fold the crepe in half. Fold it a second time to create a triangular shape. Place the crepe in the baking dish. Repeat with the remaining crepes, placing the folded crepes in the baking dish so they slightly overlap.

Sprinkle 2 tablespoons of sugar evenly over the crepes. Brown (with a blowtorch or under the broiler) until the sugar caramelizes and turns golden brown, about 5 minutes under the broiler.

GARNISH AND SERVE

Garnish by sprinkling confectioners' sugar over the crepes. Serve warm.

Sweet Coconut Tamales with Chocolate Shavings

Sweet tamales are not as well known as their savory cousins, but they are just as delicious and satisfying. Coconut and chocolate are always a good combination, but when you throw sweetened corn masa into the mix you get an unexpected symphony of flavors that seem to have been created just for this dessert. When serving them, I like to create a "tamal bar." This allows my guests to unwrap their tamales and top them with all the toasted coconut, chocolate, and cream they want.

MAKES 24 TAMALES

Dried corn husks

2^1/$_2$ cups masa harina (Maseca brand is recommended)

1 cup whole milk

1 cup coconut milk

^{3}/$_4$ cup solid vegetable shortening

^{3}/$_4$ cup sugar

1 cup unsweetened shredded coconut flakes, toasted

1 teaspoon baking powder

1 teaspoon ground cinnamon

2 teaspoons salt

^{3}/$_4$ cup Mexican crema, homemade (page 102) or store-bought

^{3}/$_4$ cup cream of coconut

Dark chocolate shavings

PREPARE THE CORN HUSKS

Soak the corn husks in simmering water for 20 minutes. They should be soft and flexible, and turn a deep beige color. Wrap the corn husks in a damp paper towel until you are ready to use them.

PREPARE THE SWEET MASA

Combine the masa harina with the whole milk and the coconut milk and mix well. The masa should have the consistency of a stiff dough. Set aside.

MAKE THE TAMAL DOUGH

Combine the shortening and sugar in a mixing bowl. Using a hand-held or standing electric mixer, beat the shortening and sugar until light and fluffy, about 3 minutes. Add a quarter of the masa to the shortening mixture and beat until well blended. Add a second quarter of the masa to the mixture and beat until well incorporated. Continue until all the masa is blended. Keep beating for another 5 minutes in order for the dough to achieve the right texture and consistency. You will know you have reached the right texture if a teaspoon of the dough floats in a cup of cold water. If after 15 minutes of constant beating your dough does not float, move on (despite it not floating, the dough will be fine).

Add ^{2}/$_3$ cup of the toasted coconut flakes to the dough along with the baking powder, cinnamon, and the salt and beat lightly until fully incorporated.

ASSEMBLE THE TAMALES

Place a corn husk lengthwise in front of you with the wide side closest to you. Spread $1/4$ cup of the dough all over the bottom half of the corn husk, leaving about a 1-inch-wide border on the left and right side. (See page 51 for photographs showing how to assemble tamales.)

Pick up the two long sides of the corn husk and unite them, forming a solid log. Roll both sides of the corn husks in the same direction over the tamal. Fold down the empty top section of the corn husk and secure it by tying a thin strip of corn husk around the tamal.

Repeat this process until all of the corn husks or tamal dough is used up.

STEAM THE TAMALES

Create a tamal steamer by crumbling a large piece of aluminum foil into a large ball and place the ball in the center of a large saucepan. Arrange the tamales "standing up" around it. You can stand tamales in front of each other, just make sure that the open end of each tamal is facing upward.

Pour in $1/2$ inch of water. Cover tightly with a lid and simmer for 40 minutes.

MAKE THE COCONUT CREAM

In a small bowl, combine the Mexican crema with the cream of coconut. (You can easily make more by combining equal amounts of each ingredient.)

SERVE

Serve the tamales warm. After opening a tamal, top with a sprinkling of shaved chocolate and some of the remaining toasted coconut flakes and drizzle with a bit of coconut cream, or let guests garnish their own. Serve extra toppings on the side.

COOKING NOTES

INGREDIENTS

Masa Harina

The flour used in tamal making is a special corn-meal that has been treated with lime and as such produces the characteristic aroma, flavor, and texture that is associated with tamales. Regular cornmeal cannot be substituted.

Cream of coconut

Do not confuse cream of coconut with coconut milk. Cream of coconut is much sweeter and thicker than the milk. (It is one of the key ingredients in piña coladas.)

TECHNIQUES

Toasting Coconut Flakes

Sprinkle the coconut flakes in single layer on a baking sheet and place in a 300°F oven. Allow to bake for about 8 minutes, or until they turn golden brown. Be on the lookout because coconut tends to burn rather quickly. However, it will send out a warning signal with the toasted coconut aroma. So as soon as you smell coconut, check on it.

Shaving Dark Chocolate

This is easily done with a bar of chocolate and a vegetable peeler. Hold the bar of chocolate with one hand (you may want to keep part of it in its wrapper so that the chocolate doesn't melt in your hands) and peel off chocolate shavings with the peeler.

ADVANCE PREPARATION

Reheating Tamales

Cooked tamales can be refrigerated for a couple of days and reheated in a steamer or in the micro-wave. If using the microwave, place the tamales in a bowl and pour in $1/4$ inch of water. Seal with plastic wrap and heat for 2 minutes. The steam created within the plastic will reheat the tamales. If reheating in a steamer, recreate the tamal steamer explained in the recipe and steam for 5 minutes.

Assembled but uncooked tamales can also be frozen. When ready to use, steam them straight from the freezer for 1 hour 20 minutes (twice the cooking time). Do not defrost before cooking.

Rice Pudding

Rice pudding is one of those desserts you want to come home to. Creamy and comforting—it's just the thing to reward yourself with at the end of a day. This classic dessert has many shortcuts, but don't fall into those traps. Really great rice pudding is not hard to make, it just takes some time and a little attention. I promise you that if you invest your time into making this dessert, you will be happy you did! **SERVES 8 TO 10**

4 cups water

$^1/_4$ cup short-grain rice (such as Arborio or Valencia)

4 cups whole milk

$^3/_4$ cup sugar

1 teaspoon vanilla extract

$^1/_4$ teaspoon salt

1 cinnamon stick, plus more for garnish

Ground cinnamon for garnish

COOKING NOTES

INGREDIENTS

Short-Grain versus Long-Grain Rice

It is best to use short-grain rice for the pudding since it is higher in starch and will produce a creamier pudding. Long-grain rice will work as well, but the texture will be slightly different.

Milk

Substituting a low-fat milk in the recipe will not produce the same creamy texture. However, feel free to substitute coconut milk (full-fat version) in equal amounts for a nice change.

TECHNIQUES

Cooking the Rice/Using Leftover Rice

In order for rice pudding to come out tender and creamy, you have to overcook the rice in an abundant amount of water. I find that using leftover rice produces a clumpy pudding with hard bits of rice. I suggest you make fresh rice specifically for this pudding and keep your leftover rice for a rice salad.

ADVANCE PREPARATION

The pudding can be made a few days in advance and kept covered in plastic wrap in the refrigerator. Place the plastic wrap directly on the surface of the pudding so that a milk skin does not form.

MAKE THE RICE

Bring the water to a boil in a saucepan. Add the rice, stir, and lower the heat to a simmer. Cook, uncovered, for 45 minutes. It will look as if all the rice grains have melted into a big clump, but they have not. The rice is just overcooked, which is what you want. Using a heatproof silicone spatula, begin stirring the rice to help the remaining water evaporate and prevent the rice and starch from sticking to the bottom of the pan. Continue until most of the liquid has evaporated. (It is impossible to get it completely dry since the starch has gelled and is holding on to some water.) Total cooking time will be about 1 hour.

Turn off the heat.

BOIL THE MILK

Combine the milk, sugar, vanilla, salt, and cinnamon stick in a saucepan and bring to a boil.

COMBINE THE MILK AND RICE

Pour the boiling milk mixture into the rice, stir well, and turn on the heat to medium. It will seem as if you have added too much milk, but you have not.

Cook the rice, stirring every 5 minutes or so to remove the skin that forms and the starch that builds up along the side of the pan, until the liquid is reduced by half. This should take about 45 minutes.

This step does require you to stay in close range of the pan because leaving it unattended can cause the milk to boil over. Stirring also helps speed the evaporation process because it prevents a skin from forming on the surface of the pan (which would keep the steam from escaping).

The pudding will thicken as it cools, so keep that in mind when judging the consistency.

GARNISH AND SERVE

You can serve the rice hot, chilled, or at room temperature. Garnish each serving with a sprinkling of ground cinnamon and a cinnamon stick, if you like.

Fried Caramelized Bananas with Ice Cream

I like to think of this as a Mexican banana split, which isn't as crazy as it sounds when you realize how important and prevalent ice cream is in Mexico. Quick, easy, and irresistible—you will have this dessert on the table faster than anyone can eat it, which is quite a statement considering how unbelievably mouth-watering it is. **SERVES 6**

1/2 cup light brown sugar, firmly packed

4 tablespoons unsalted butter

3 bananas, peeled and halved lengthwise

1/4 cup chopped pecans

1 pint vanilla ice cream

COOKING NOTES

ADVANCE PREPARATION

The bananas are best served just after they are made. They will lose their crispy caramelized texture as they sit but will still retain their flavor so long as they are not refrigerated.

If you must make them in advance, the bananas can be held in a warm oven for a few hours.

MAKE THE CARAMEL

Place a nonstick skillet over medium-high heat and add the brown sugar and butter. Allow both to melt and mix well using a heatproof silicone spatula.

FRY THE BANANAS

When the caramel is hot and bubbly, add the bananas, cut side down, along with the pecans. Allow the bananas to cook for about 3 minutes before turning them over. The cut side should have a deep golden brown color and a slightly crispy texture. (Depending on the ripeness of the banana, they may break. Don't worry about this; they will still be delicious.)

Cook for another 2 minutes, using a spoon to drizzle the caramel sauce over the bananas to keep infusing them with caramel flavor.

SERVE

Place the bananas on a serving dish or platter, top with scoops of ice cream, and drizzle the caramel sauce and nuts all over it.

Index

To my parents, Alina, Fausto, Georgina, and Alfredo, who always support me, even when they don't understand me.

Acknowledgments

Simple and authentic not only describes this book, but also its writing process. From the time the project was first discussed to its publication, everything seemed to flow. I've been told this is not always the case and so I can only attribute it to the people who took part in its formation. From the bottom of my heart, thank you!

MANY THANKS AND MUCH GRATITUDE

To those at Ten Speed Press: Lorena Jones for giving me the opportunity (and gift) to do what I love; Melissa Moore for your cross-country guidance and ridiculously easygoing nature; Nancy Austin for your organic approach and great visual style.

To the best photography team: Lucy Schaeffer for bringing the book to life with your brilliant photography; Shane Walsh for putting that killer smile on my face; Penelope Bouklas for your gorgeous styling and spirit; Rachel Schwab for your enthusiasm and invaluable assistance.

To my agent and friends: Bob Silverstein for walking me through this experience and finding the perfect home at Ten Speed Press; David Rosengarten for taking the time to set me in the right direction; Aarón Sánchez for answering all my questions and making sure everything stayed authentic.

MUCH LOVE AND APPRECIATION

To my sisters and brothers-in-law, Alina, Ozzie, Yvi, and Manny, for being the best tasters and encouraging my impromptu meals at your home; to all the students I have had the pleasure of teaching for keeping me on my toes and constantly inspiring me!

10

Ten Speed Press
PO Box 7123
Berkeley, California 94707
www.tenspeed.com

Distributed in Australia by Simon and Schuster Australia, in Canada by Ten Speed Press Canada,
in New Zealand by Southern Publishers Group, in South Africa by Real Books, and in the United
Kingdom and Europe by Publishers Group UK.

Cover and text design by Nancy Austin
Prop styling by Penelope Bouklas for Halley Resources

Library of Congress Cataloging-in-Publication Data
Castro, Lourdes.
  Simply Mexican / Lourdes Castro ; photography by Lucy Schaeffer.
    p. cm.
  Includes index.
  Summary: "A solid, accessible introduction to Mexican cooking featuring 60 easy and authentic
recipes for quick-to-the-table meals; each recipe includes 'Cooking Notes' that highlight equip-
ment, ingredients, techniques, and instructions for advance preparation"—Provided by publisher.
  ISBN 978-1-58008-952-4
  1. Cookery, Mexican. 2. Quick and easy cookery. I. Title.
  TX716.M4C3978 2009
  641.5972—dc22

                        2008042072

Printed in China
First printing, 2009
1 2 3 4 5 6 7 8 9 10 — 13 12 11 10 09